•COMPUTER CLUB•

BIRDWATCH

Text:
Chris Harbard & Tim Stowe

Programs:
Pinewood Programming

Macdonald

A MACDONALD BOOK

© Macdonald & Co (Publishers) 1984

First published in Great Britain in 1984
by Macdonald & Co (Publishers) Ltd

A BPCC plc Company

ISBN 0 356 11021 4

Printed and bound in Belgium
by Henri Proost

Macdonald & Co (Publishers) Ltd
Maxwell House
74 Worship Street
London EC2A 2EN

Editor
Daphne Butler

Production
Rosemary Bishop

Picture Research
Kathy Lockley

Consultants
Derrick Daines
Crispin Fisher

Teacher Panel
Wendy Cunningham
Debbie Twineham

Design Concept
Sally Henry

Book Design
Richard Garratt

Illustrators
Mike Hodgson
Raymond Turvey
Paula Youens

Photographs
J A Bailey/Ardea   28
A C Clay/RSPB   40–41
Bruce Coleman   7, 41
Stephen Dalton/NHPA   6
Ian Griffiths/Robert Harding   7
Robert Harding *Front cover*
Roger Hosking   32
Macdonald/Fiona Pragoff   34
C J Smale/Aquila   14–15
Walter Rawlings/Robert Harding   36
M W Richards/RSPB   40
Annie Wilkin/NHPA   26
ZEFA   29

Stowe, Tim
   Birdwatch.—(Computer club)
   1. Ornithology—Data processing—
   Juvenile literature
   I. Title II. Harbard, Chris III. Series
   598′.028′54   QL676.2

ISBN 0-356-11021-4

About this book

There are three different ways in which you can use this book. One way is to use it to find out more about birdwatching. A second way is to use the programs and information to carry out bird projects with a microcomputer. The third way is to use the programs to develop your computer skills. Projects for the computer are on pages with a blue border. Each project is positioned in the book next to bird information needed for the program.

About the programs

The programs are written in structured BASIC for the BBC microcomputer, and are designed to be changed and adapted. Each project page has a description of the program, a listing of the program, and suggestions for changes you can make.

Start by reading the description and then type the program in at the keyboard of your computer. The program must be copied exactly. It is very likely that you will make mistakes and before the program will run it must be debugged.

When the program is running properly you can use it as part of a bird project. You can also try out the program changes suggested after the program listing. Perhaps you can invent your own modifications.

The programs can be saved on disc or cassette, copied, and given to your friends, but under no circumstances may you sell them.

A cassette tape containing the programs in this book is available for the BBC Model B and the Spectrum 48k.

For the absolute beginner

Before trying to use the programs please get a knowledgeable adult or friend to teach you the following things:

How to use the keyboard.
How to type in and run a program.
How to save a program on cassette tape.
How to load a program from cassette tape.

BIRDWATCH

Contents

★Pages containing computer programs, data,
or hints for using your microcomputer
are enclosed in stars★

Birds all around

Wherever you look, at home or at school, in the country or towns, you will find birds. Some are obvious, flying overhead or feeding at the bird table. Others are secretive and shy away when people come near, but all can be seen if you look carefully. Even in our largest cities birds such as sparrows and pigeons have found a place to live. They feed during the day on scraps left by people and sleep at night on buildings. More unusual birds like the kestrel can also be found, feeding over parks and resting on tall buildings.

Watching birds

Watching birds is fascinating. There is so much to discover about how many there are, what they do, and how and where they breed. Some birds stay all the year round, whilst others are only seen in spring and summer. Others only visit in winter. Throughout the year the number and kind of birds around us changes. So, whatever time of year you watch birds there is always something interesting or different to see.

You will be amazed at the variety of shapes, sizes and colours of birds. Even common birds like blue tits and robins are brightly coloured. Others are nearly all black like blackbirds and rooks, or nearly pure white like swans. Perhaps birds are most fascinating because they can fly, something humans have never been able to do without the help of machines.

To watch birds you need to have a sharp pair of eyes. The knowledge people have of birds lies in careful observation. The first ornithologists, people who study birds, did not even have binoculars. Today binoculars, telescopes, radio-tracking equipment and computers are all used. This book tries to show you how a microcomputer, at home or at school, can help you as you learn more about birds.

In winter many species of birds will visit a bird table, attracted by a variety of foods.

In spring many birds can be encouraged to stay and breed in carefully sited nestboxes.

Using a computer to record observations can aid understanding of the habits of birds.

A pond will attract birds throughout the year, whether to drink or to bathe.

What is a bird?

Birds have been on the Earth for about 150 million years, and evolved from reptiles which probably lived in trees. The scales of the reptiles were probably enlarged to help them to glide between the trees, and they would have fed on insects.

The earliest bird known is *Archaeopteryx* which still had many reptilian features but possessed something unique to birds: feathers. As birds continued to evolve their bones became lighter, their wings stronger, and eventually true flight was achieved. Birds' bones are so light because they are hollow or contain an honeycomb structure.

Feathers, like hair, are made of keratin and consist of a stiff central shaft with a vane of barbs on each side. The barbs are linked by barbules which form a continuous surface. Feathers not only enable birds to fly but also provide protection and warmth. Feathers may be coloured to provide camouflage and may be brightly coloured for courtship displays, perhaps both. Males of most species are usually more highly coloured than females.

Wing and tail feathers are long and broad to provide the maximum resistance to the air. When a wing moves upwards, the feathers can separate to allow the air to pass between them, and on the down stroke they overlap giving a surface to push against the air, lifting the bird and propelling it forwards.

Because feathers wear they must be replaced in a process called moulting. This normally happens gradually so that the birds can still fly. Ducks and some other waterbirds do become flightless for a time. The renewal of feathers normally takes place after breeding. Some birds however will moult some of their feathers to change from their winter plumage into their breeding plumage.

Not all birds are able to fly. Ostriches of Africa have taken to living on the ground and are fast runners. Penguins have adapted to life in the sea.

◄ Archaeopteryx *was a prototype bird, and still possessed many reptilian features such as clawed wings, a long bony tail, and a toothed beak.*

▲ *An enlarged picture of a feather showing a central shaft with barbs, each connected to the next by hooked barbules.*
A little owl displays its parted feathers and angled wing on the upstroke and overlapping feathers and horizontal wing on the downstroke. ▼

Bird names

The names we have given to birds are derived from many different languages. At one time a bird would be called something different in each region of the country. The lapwing, named after its flight, was also called the peewit after its call and the green plover after its appearance. The kestrel, a familiar bird near motorways, was also known as the windhover because of its method of finding prey.

Many names are descriptive in some way and communicate something about the nature of the bird. Some birds are named after where they are found: house sparrows near buildings, and fieldfares in fields. The size of a bird often becomes part of a name: the great tit is bigger than other tits, and the little grebe is our smallest grebe. Blackbirds and greenfinches are named after their chief colours. Blackcaps have a black cap, and crossbills have specially adapted crossed bills for extracting seeds from pinecones. Nuthatches are named after one of their foods, as is the kingfisher. A name may describe a bird's behaviour: treecreepers climb up trees, and swifts are very fast fliers. A bird's song or voice is often imitated by its name. We all know a cuckoo when we hear one, and anyone hearing a kittiwake, a cliff-nesting gull, would recognise it just as easily by the same means.

Bird families

Closely related birds often have group names, rather like a surname. The greenfinch and the hawfinch are both members of

▲ *A male crossbill, named after its peculiar bill which is adapted to enable it to remove seeds from pine cones.*

A young great spotted woodpecker which is already larger than the lesser spotted woodpecker can be attracted to a bird feeder containing peanuts. ▼

the finch family, marsh tits and great tits are both members of the tit family. Sometimes the links are not indicated by the name. Without seeing them you would not realise that blackbirds, redwings and song thrushes are all members of the thrush family.

To describe the relationships between different types of birds a new set of *scientific* names is needed. The names are derived from Latin and Greek and are in two parts. The first name or generic name describes the group or genus to which the bird belongs. The second or specific name describes the individual bird or species. These names are recognized internationally and enable you to describe a bird species to anyone whatever language they may speak.

Habitat	House sparrow	Marsh tit	Fieldfare
Size	Great tit	Little grebe	Great spotted woodpecker
Colour	Blackbird	Greenfinch	Yellowhammer
Appearance	Blackcap	Crossbill	Redwing
Food	Nuthatch	Hawfinch	Kingfisher
Behaviour	Swift	Treecreeper	Dipper
Voice	Cuckoo	Chiffchaff	Kittiwake

Program: ANAGRAMS

This program is an anagram game based on the names of birds. On the screen you will see a bird's name with the letters in the wrong order. You must type in the correct name, and then press RETURN. *If you get the answer wrong the program will tell you the right answer. After ten questions you will be told your score and the time you took altogether. Run the program with the* CAPS LOCK *off. Type the program in at the keyboard and debug it so that it runs properly. Save the program on cassette.*

```
 10 MODE7
 20 VDU23;8202;0;0;0;
 30 DIM B(15),A(10)
 40 SCORE=0
 50 Q=10
 60 TIME=0
 70 FOR QUESTION=1 TO Q
 80    CLS
 90    PROCDOUBLE("Anagram : "+STR$(QUE
STION),2,2,133)
100    PROCDOUBLE("Score : "+STR$(SCORE
),24,2,133)
110    PRINT TAB(1,23)CHR$131"Play this
 game with CAPS LOCK off."
120    PROCPICKABIRD
130    PROCANAGRAM
140    PROCQUESTION
150    NEXT QUESTION
160 FOR C=0 TO 20
170    PRINT TAB(0,C) CHR$135 CHR$157 "
180    NEXT C
190 PROCDOUBLE("SCORE = "+STR$(SCORE)+
" out of "+STR$(Q),9,7,129)
200 PROCDOUBLE("TIME = "+STR$(INT(TIME
/100+.5))+" seconds",10,12,129)
210 PRINT TAB(1,23)CHR$131"      Press
any key to play again.   "
220 *FX15,0
230 A=GET
240 RUN
250 END

260 DEFPROCPICKABIRD
270 DATAfieldfare,blackbird,magpie,gol
dcrest,jackdaw,redwing,nuthatch,hawfinch
,raven,swift,robin,cuckoo,kittiwake,swal
low,jay
280 RESTORE 270
290 R=RND(15)
300 IF B(R)<>0 THEN GOTO 290
310 FOR N=1 TO R
320    READ BIRD$
330    NEXT N
340 B(R)=1
350 ENDPROC
```

```
360 DEFPROCANAGRAM
370 FOR E=1 TO 10
380    A(E)=0
390    NEXT E
400 ANAG$=""
410 L=LEN(BIRD$)
420 FOR N=1 TO L
430    B=RND(L)
440    IF A(B)<>0 THEN GOTO 430
450    ANAG$=ANAG$+MID$(BIRD$,B,1)
460    A(B)=1
470    NEXT N
480 IF ANAG$=BIRD$ THEN GOTO370
490 ENDPROC

500 DEFPROCQUESTION
510 PROCDOUBLE(ANAG$,15,7,135)
520 *FX15,0
530 INPUT TAB(1,12)"Name the bird - "
ANSWER$
540 IF RIGHT$(ANSWER$,1)=" " THEN REPE
AT:L=LEN ANSWER$:ANSWER$=LEFT$(ANSWER$,L
-1):UNTIL RIGHT$(ANSWER$,1)<>" "
550 IF ANSWER$=BIRD$ THEN PROCDOUBLE("
CORRECT,",0,15,130):SCORE=SCORE+1 ELSE P
ROCDOUBLE("WRONG ,",0,15,129)
560 PRINTTAB(9,17) "it is a "
570 PROCDOUBLE(BIRD$+".",15,18,133)
580 PROCDOUBLE("Score : "+STR$(SCORE),
24,2,133)
590 FOR N=1 TO 5000
600    NEXT N
610 ENDPROC

620 DEFPROCDOUBLE(T$,C,L,COL)
630 PRINT TAB(C,L)CHR$141 CHR$(COL)T$
TAB(C,L+1)CHR$141 CHR$(COL) T$
640 ENDPROC
```

Try these changes

1. Change the number of questions by changing the value of Q in line 50. Do not make Q greater than the number of names in the DATA at line 270.

2. Try making a game for your friends by changing the DATA. There are 15 names in the DATA at line 270. You can change the names, but if any are longer than 10 letters you must change the 10 in these lines:

```
30 DIM B(15),A(10)
370 FOR E=1 TO 10
```

If you increase the number of names in the DATA, you must also change the 15 in these lines:

```
30 DIM B(15),A(10)
290 R=RND(15)
```

3. Try making the program give the time in minutes and seconds. You will need the commands MOD60 and DIV60, and the BBC User Manual.

Shapes and parts

▲ *A male house sparrow shows many of the features that should be noted when you try to describe and identify a bird.*

The shape of a bird is determined by the way it lives, in particular the need to fly. To reduce air resistance in flight the head is usually small and the body streamlined. At rest the wings are not needed and fold neatly against the sides of the body. Most birds are seen best when they are stationary. Describing their different shapes and parts will help you identify them.

To make a sketch of a bird is fairly easy and can be done on the computer. Try the program SketchB on page 10. The computer picture is obviously a bird, but which species is it? See how different birds have different shapes. The way birds stand is often a useful clue to their identity. Land-dwelling birds have their legs in the middle of their body and usually stand with their bodies held horizontally. Water-dwelling birds have their legs further back towards the end of their body; they can swim well but walk only with difficulty and need to sit or stand upright out of

the water. Birds that spend most of their time flying, like swifts and swallows, are more streamlined than those that spend most of their time on the ground like pheasants and partridges. Look at the shapes of birds pictured in this book.

To identify a bird further you will need to look at the parts of the bird shown in the illustrations and in the computer drawing. Note the length of the bill, legs and tail. The tail and wing feathers and the wing coverts often carry distinctive markings which will help you identify it. All birds have excellent hearing but you cannot

see the ears themselves; they are hidden under the ear coverts. If you see a bird you cannot identify, compare its size to a bird that you know such as a sparrow or pigeon and note the colour and shape of the parts labelled in the drawing. If you do this accurately, and then compare it with the illustrations in a field guide, you should be able to identify any species.

Program: SKETCHB

The aim of this program is to help you to draw birds and to show you some program editing. When trying to draw an object it is easiest to sketch in its basic outline first. This way you get the proportions right.

SketchB produces a simple outline for a bird which you can change to draw your own bird. You may like to trace the outline from the television or monitor by fixing tracing paper over the screen.

The basic outline

```
 10 MODE1
 20 VDU23;8202;0;0;0;
 30 COLOUR129:CLS

 40 REM      **   Head   **
 50 PROCOVAL(260,670,100,60,0)

 60 REM      **   Bill   **
 70 MOVE160,672:DRAW80,672

 80 REM      **   Eye    **
 90 PRINT TAB(7,10)"o"

100 REM      **   Body   **
110 PROCOVAL(630,480,250,100,0)

120 REM      **   Neck   **
130 MOVE420,540:DRAW350,645

140 REM      **   Tail   **
150 MOVE862,512:DRAW1212,562

160 REM **   Primaries+Secondaries
**
170 MOVE830,464:DRAW950,424:DRAW7
00,444

180 REM      **   Leg    **
190 MOVE654,376:DRAW684,326:DRAW6
34,176

200 REM      **   Toes   **
210 DRAW530,176:DRAW680,176
```

```
220 PRINT TAB(2,30)"Press SPACE B
AR to clear the screen."
230 *FX15,0
240 REPEAT:UNTIL GET=32
250 CLS:END

260 DEFPROCOVAL(X,Y,S1%,S2%,T)
270 T=T*PI/6-PI/2
280 VDU29,X;Y;
290 MOVE S2%*COS T,-S2%*SIN T
300 FOR D=0 TO 2*PI STEP PI/30
310    DRAW S2%*COS D*COS T+S1%*SI
N D*SIN T,-S2%*COS D*SIN T+S1%*SIN
D*COS T
320    NEXT
330 VDU29,0;0;
340 ENDPROC
```

When you have debugged the basic outline program, so that it runs properly, save it on cassette.

Make a duck

Load the basic outline from cassette and type in the lines below at the keyboard. The computer will insert the lines into the program automatically. The program will now draw a duck for you.

```
 50 PROCOVAL(368,680,100,60,0)

 70 MOVE272,696:DRAW256,648:DRAW1
84,600:DRAW304,632

 90 PRINT TAB(10,10)"o"

110 PROCOVAL(560,368,320,120,.5)

130 MOVE288,488:DRAW352,616:MOVE4
32,632:DRAW408,512

150 MOVE752,224:DRAW928,224:DRAW9
04,264

170 MOVE832,360:DRAW992,248:DRAW7
84,288

190 MOVE632,232:DRAW632,144

210 DRAW488,144
```

Make your own bird

The program can be used to design a simple outline for any bird. For this you use a special procedure to edit the main program. The procedure is called PROCCOORDS and it links on to the end of the basic outline program.

Load the basic outline into the computer and then key in PROCCOORDS. If you have the Birdwatch cassette this procedure is already included in SketchB.

```
350 DEFPROCCOORDS
360 VDU30:PRINT" PROCCOORDS: PRES
S SPACE BAR TO LEAVE."
370 IF X%>1271 OR X%<0 THEN X%=0
380 IF Y%>919 OR Y%<0 THEN Y%=0
390 VDU19,0,8,0,0,0
400 GCOL0,129:GCOL0,0
410 *FX4,1
420 VDU29,0;0;
430 REPEAT
440    S=0:IF POINT(X%,Y%)=3 THEN
S=1
450    PLOT 69,X%,Y%
460    A=GET
470    NX%=X%-8*(A=&89 AND X%<1272
)+8*(A=&88 AND X%>7)
480    NY%=Y%-8*(A=&8B AND Y%<920)
+8*(A=&8A AND Y%>7)
490    IF NX%=X% AND NY%=Y% AND A<
>32 THEN 460
500    IF S=0 THEN PLOT 71,X%,Y% E
LSE PLOT 70,X%,Y%
510    X%=NX%:Y%=NY%
520    PRINT TAB(13,2)"X=";X%;"  :
Y="Y%"           "
530    UNTIL A=32
540 GCOL0,3:VDU30:PRINT STRING$(1
20," ")
550 *FX4,0
560 ENDPROC
```

Now type

```
*KEY 0 PROCCOORDS¦M
```

and press RETURN. *(In MODE 7* ¦ *is shown on the screen as* ‖ *.)*
This defines the red key f0 *so that any time you need to use*
PROCCOORDS *all you need to do is press* f0.

Using PROCCOORDS
To design your own bird using PROCCOORDS *follow the*
steps below. PROCCOORDS *is a procedure which helps you to*
locate any point on the screen. You must press the SPACE BAR
every time you have finished using PROCCOORDS.

Changing the head
1. Insert into the program,
35 END

2. Run the program.

3. Press red key f0 *for* PROCCOORDS.
A tiny flashing dot will appear in the bottom left hand corner of
the screen (or if you have already used PROCCOORDS *the dot*
will be where you left it). Using the cursor keys move the dot to
to where you would like the centre of your bird's head to be.
Write down on a piece of paper the numbers for X *and* Y *which*
you will see at the top of the screen.
Press the SPACE BAR *to leave* PROCCOORDS.

4. Insert into the program, 50 PROCOVAL (X,Y,100,60,0)
For X *and* Y *use the numbers which you wrote on your piece of*
paper.

5. Remove line 35 and insert line 55 END *so that the program*
will end after the head has been drawn. To remove a line type
the line number and press RETURN.

6. Run the program. If the position of the head is not right go
back to step 1. If you do not like the shape of your bird's head
change line 50. If you wish to change the length of the head
change the third number; if you wish to change the width,
change the fourth number; if you wish to change the tilt, change
the last number. The tilt can have any value between 0 and 6. Do
not be afraid to experiment.

Changing the bill
1. Make sure that line 55 END *is inserted in program.*

2. Run the program and the head will be drawn on the screen.

3. Press red key f0 *for* PROCCOORDS.
Using the cursor keys move the dot to where you want the head-
end of the bill to be. Write down the numbers X *and* Y. *Move*
the dot to where you want the point of the bill to be and write
down the values of X *and* Y *again. Press the*
SPACE BAR *to leave* PROCCOORDS.

4. Insert into the program
70 MOVEX,Y: DRAWX,Y
After MOVE *use the numbers for the head-end of the bill and*
after DRAW *use the numbers for the point.*

5. Remove line 55 END *and insert line 75* END *so that when you*
run the program it will end after the head and the bill have
been drawn.

6. Run the program. The head and the bill of your bird will
be drawn on the screen. The bill will appear as a single line.
If you want to change the bill go back to step 1 and try again.

Changing the eye
1. Make sure that line 75 END *is inserted in program.*

2. Run the program.
The head and the bill will appear on the screen. The width of
the screen is 40 units, estimate how far across you need to put
the eye. The depth of the screen is 32 units, estimate how far
down you need to put the eye. Write down both estimates on a
piece of paper.

3. Insert into the program
90 PRINT TAB (W,D)"o"
For W *use your estimate for the width. For* D *use your estimate*
for the depth.

4. Remove line 75 and insert line 95 END *so that the program*
will end after it has drawn the head, the bill and the eye.

5. Run the program. Continue to experiment until the eye is in
the right position.

Using similar steps work through the program changing the rest
of the bird. Remember that whenever you need to know the
position of a point on the screen press red key f0 *for*
PROCCOORDS. *The body uses the same method as the head.*
The remainder of the bird uses the same method as the bill.

Identification

The parts of a bird will tell you something about how the bird lives as well as helping you identify it.

Bill for food

Birds feed in a variety of ways, and their bill shapes reflect this. Seed eating birds have short, stubby bills to break the seeds open. Insect eating birds have thin, delicate bills to pick at insects. Wading birds which feed by probing their bills into the ground have long and thin bills.

Legs and feet

Wading birds have long legs to allow them to feed in water and keep dry; an easy feature to see in the field. You need to be closer to birds to see their feet. Most garden birds have feet for perching, with three toes pointing forward and one backward. Woodpeckers have two pointing forward and two pointing back to help them to climb trees. The feet of birds of prey are equipped with sharp talons to grip their prey whilst birds that live in water have webbed feet that act like paddles.

Wings

In flight many birds have distinctive wing shapes and colours. These are not always easy to see so do not be put off if you cannot always see them. Fast flying birds have pointed wings. Birds that need to take off quickly but only fly short distances, such as pheasants, have broad, rounded wings. Many birds have the wing

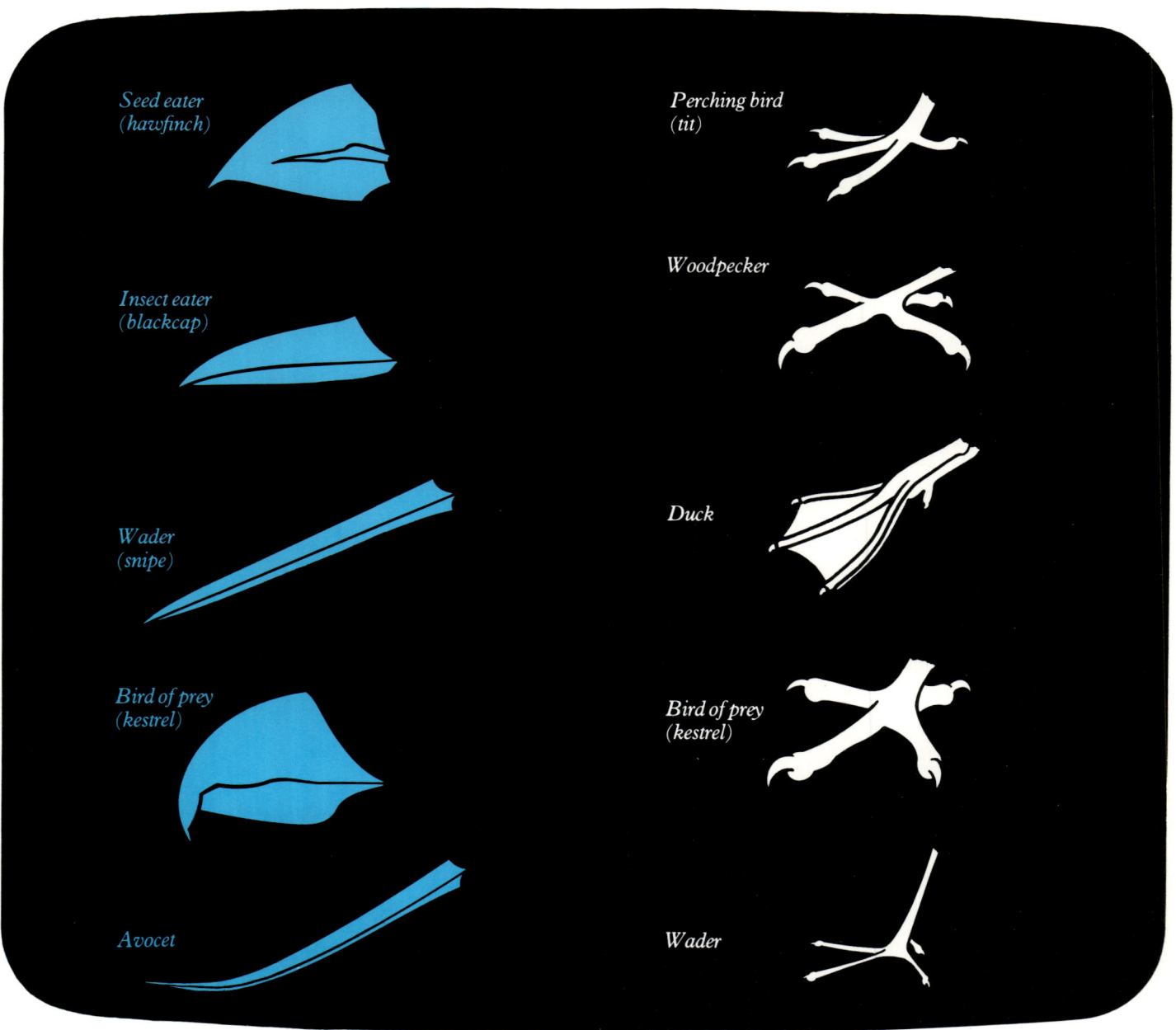

Seed eater (hawfinch)

Insect eater (blackcap)

Wader (snipe)

Bird of prey (kestrel)

Avocet

Perching bird (tit)

Woodpecker

Duck

Bird of prey (kestrel)

Wader

coverts tipped white forming a distinctive wing bar.

Tails

The tail feathers are used to help a bird remain stable in flight. The shape and colour of the tail are a useful aid to identification. For example the female kestrel has a barred reddish brown tail. The male's is grey with a black band near the tip. Woodpeckers use their tails to support them against the tree so the feathers are specially strengthened.

Behaviour and flight

The behaviour of a bird can also give you a clue to its identity. Some ducks dive to catch their food, others up-end on the surface. In flight birds such as finches or woodpeckers have undulating flight. Herons have a level flight whilst lapwings swoop and tumble in display flight. Buzzards soar, circling, whilst kestrels hover, hunting. Most birds of prey are solitary. Other birds like gulls, woodpigeons and starlings form flocks.

Songs and calls

Most people know the cuckoo's call or the hoot of a tawny owl. With experience you will be able to tell other birds by their song. Woodpeckers give away their presence by drumming. This sound is not produced inside the bird but by hammering the bill hard against a tree. If you see swans flying near listen for the sound of their wings.

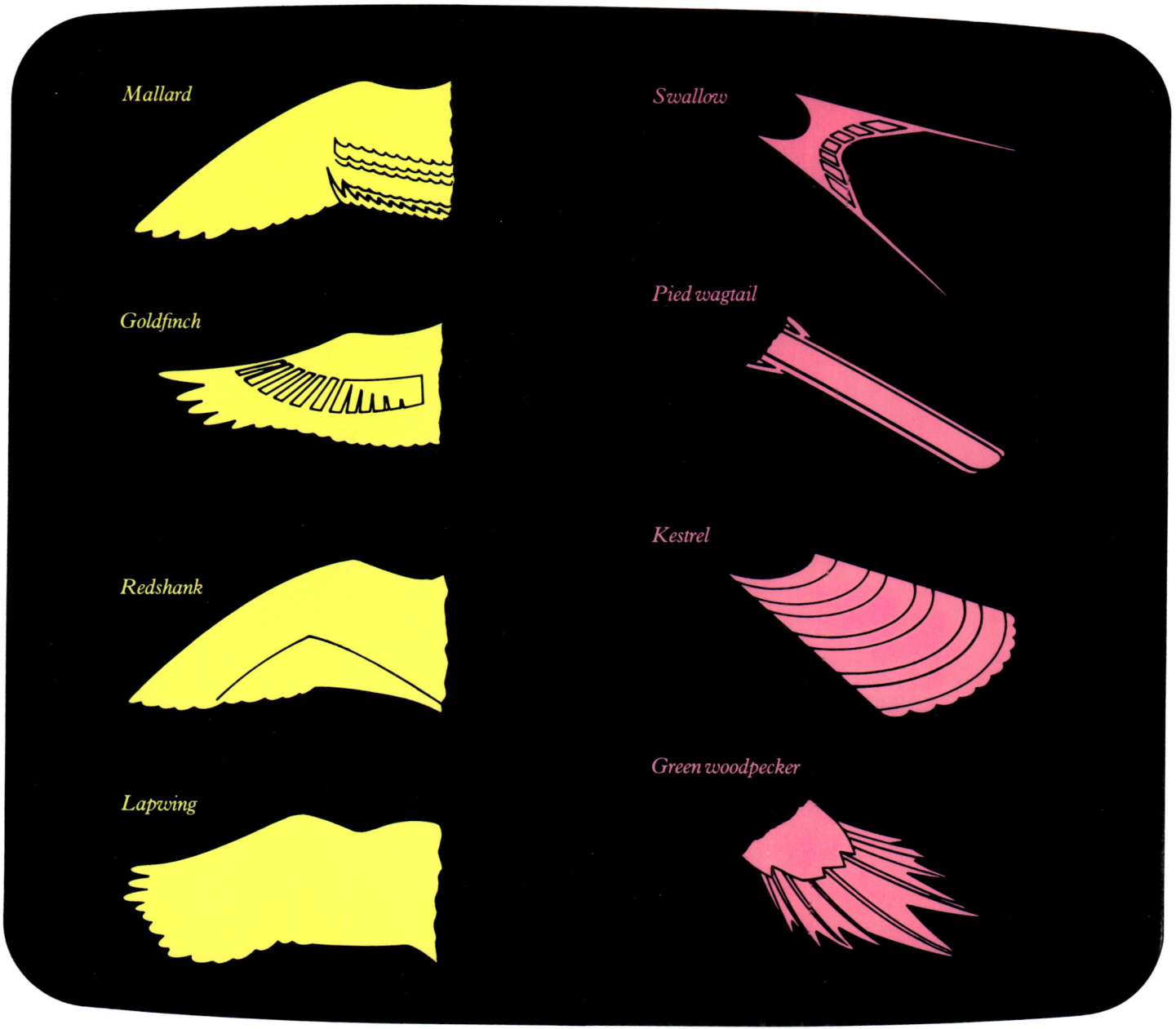

Mallard

Goldfinch

Redshank

Lapwing

Swallow

Pied wagtail

Kestrel

Green woodpecker

How and where

How to watch

Birds can be watched anywhere. You can study them without using any special equipment, but for detailed study you will need binoculars. There are many different makes of binocular and you should always try out several pairs before purchasing to make sure they are not too heavy and that you can use them with ease.

The best magnifications to use are between 8x and 10x.

The next requirement is a notebook for making notes. A small pocket book is best and your notes can be transferred to your computer later.

You should wear clothing that is inconspicuous. Do not wear brightly coloured anoraks, and in winter make sure your clothing is warm, windproof, and waterproof.

To learn about birds you need to watch them. Although field guides and other books are useful, experience in the field is the only way to learn. One way to gain this is to join a local birdwatching club or a local Young Ornithologists' Club which hold regular meetings and outings and involve members in projects.

Lastly always remember to remain quiet and not to disturb

birds because birds soon get used to them and are not aware of the watchers inside. A car can be used as a hide if it is parked carefully and quietly.

Where to watch

Gardens will have only a limited variety of birds. To see a wider range of species you will need to travel further afield.

A local park with a lake can be a good place to start; you could see mallard, moorhen, black-headed gull. Woodland, especially deciduous, will contain warblers, woodpeckers, tits and finches. A reservoir or gravel pit will attract ducks and other waterbirds, estuaries and marshes will be good for wading birds. If you are near the coast you will have an opportunity to watch seabirds.

Nature reserves are good places to visit; you can be sure they will be interesting. The hides provide good views of the birds and you will have an opportunity to meet other birdwatchers.

Wherever you birdwatch, always ensure that you have permission to be there. Local woods, fields and gravel pits will probably be privately owned. Always follow a public right of way. Always take care to follow the Country Code, and if you are birdwatching on a tidal estuary take care not to get caught by the tide

Dawn is the best time to watch birds, particularly in spring when they are very active.

▲ *Estuaries are a good place to see wading birds such as dunlin and bar-tailed godwit as they travel to their breeding and wintering grounds.*

Always dress correctly and ▲ *inconspicuously when watching birds as they will also be keeping an eye out for you.*

the bird you want to watch. Patient sitting and waiting will always be rewarding; noisy and hurried movements will only frighten the birds away. When approaching a bird, use bushes and trees or a rise in the ground to conceal you. Hides are excellent for getting close to

Keeping notes

Home → School   17th April
8:30 a.m. Sunny
1 Swallow - Mill pond
2 Mistle Thrush (one in song)
1 Robin
2 Magpie
1 Song Thrush (singing)
Starling
1 Chaffinch
Lapwing - 'Big field': Display
Heron - flying NNW.
Dunnock - School : display
Pied Wagtail - School
3 House Martins (above school)
1 Kestrel (school fields)

Whenever you watch birds, you will want to record your observations. Make your notes carefully and immediately, otherwise you will forget the detail of what you have seen within a few minutes. Remember that your observations are unrepeatable and if not properly recorded they will be lost forever. Carry a notebook that will fit into your pocket and a pencil (ink runs in the wet). Write your name and address on the inside cover of the notebook. A looseleaf notebook is useful because at the end of each day you can remove the notes and type the information onto the computer. The sheets can then be stored in another file for safety, leaving a clean book for the next day's notes. This way, if you should ever lose your book you will not lose all your notes.

Before you start watching remember to note down the date,

the time, and the weather conditions. The weather is important because it affects how the birds behave, particularly how often they sing. It also affects how well you see them. In windy or rainy conditions your powers of observation can be badly affected. Make a note of the temperature and whether the wind is light, moderate or strong. The extent of cloud cover is also worth recording. The conventional way to do this is to measure it in eighths: 0/8 for clear skies up to 8/8 for completely overcast. When you have made several observations in the same place in different weather conditions, compare the numbers and species of birds you have seen.

If you are counting large numbers of birds make a list of species and mark each time you see a bird, marking off units of five. Do not be tempted to abbreviate names or other

notes unless you are certain you will remember what they mean when you come to put them on the computer.

Sometimes you will see a bird you cannot identify. Note the time and place and the habitat, and draw a simple outline of the bird. Put on any distinctive markings and describe the main colours and the behaviour. Beneath the sketch list the shape, size and colour of the main parts of the bird as described on page 9. In case you cannot remember what parts to look at carry a list of them on the first page of your notebook.

When you have put your notes on the computer or identified your mystery bird, do not throw your notes away. You may want to refer to them one day, or pass some of your sightings to the local bird recorder. Each region has a bird recorder who collates records from all birdwatchers at the end of each year. The records are usually published in an annual report. If you have seen something unusual you should send a full description to the recorder.

Robin singing

Make notes of bird behaviour in your notebook.

Chaffinch preening

Blackbird feeding

16

USING A DATABASE

A database is a simple means of storing information on a computer. You can search through the database and recall some, or all of it, in a variety of ways. You can also add to it and change it. There are several database programs available for microcomputers. The software list on page 47 makes some suggestions.

A suitable subject

Suppose you have made counts of numbers of birds at a bird table, and recorded the number of times four different foods were eaten. To use a database program you will first have to decide what categories or headings you want to store the information under. You will need to make the first heading the bird *species*. The second heading will be the *number* of each species. Then you will need a separate heading for each food type, say *peanuts*, *biscuit*, *raisins* and *apples*. As a final heading you could put the *date* so you know when you saw the birds. The database program will ask you to enter your headings.

Database asks for	You type in
Heading 1	*Species*
Heading 2	*Number seen*
Heading 3	*Peanuts*
Heading 4	*Biscuit*
Heading 5	*Raisins*
Heading 6	*Apples*
Heading 7	*Date*

Entering your data

Once you have decided on your headings and entered them you can enter the data from the observations you have made. Suppose you saw blue tits at your bird table. You will need to enter your blue tit data under each heading in turn. If a food was not eaten then do not make an entry.

Database asks for	You type in
Species	*Blue tit*
Number seen	*10*
Peanuts	*8*
Biscuit	*2*
Raisins	
Apples	
Date	*10 December*

You should enter the data for every species of bird you observed.

Using the information

When all the information has been entered and stored you can use the database to answer questions about the information you have given to it. You might wish to know which bird came to the bird table most often on that day. To do this you must ask for the highest number seen and the species corresponding to that number.

The usefulness of the database increases as you put more information in. If you continue to add to your database for a whole month you will be able to produce a table like that one on page 20 under *Presenting results*. To do this you will have to ask the database for all the information on numbers and food eaten for a particular species.

You may wish to add an extra heading to your database at some time, for example weather. You will need to pick meaningful entries to describe the conditions, for instance, mild, cold, stormy. Separate headings for temperature and wind strength could be used. This would allow you to discover how the weather affects the numbers or species of bird feeding or the type of food eaten. Try working out how you might get this information from the computer.

What to study

Feeding

The easiest way to study birds is to attract them to your garden or school by putting out food on a bird table. Please remember that you should not feed birds during the breeding season. There are plenty of natural foods available providing a balanced diet. Bird table food could also be dangerous, peanuts fed to baby birds could choke them. Put out a selection of foods and watch for 15 minutes once a day or a week. Find out how many species come to feed. Watch each species in turn and record the highest number that visit at the same time. Do the numbers change over the winter or with the weather conditions?

Do some birds seem to prefer some foods to others? Put out several different foods in similar amounts and record how often each species feeds on each food. If you spend ten minutes per day doing this for a month you will have a good idea of which foods attract which species.

Find out whether birds feed more frequently at different times of the day. Count the number of each species feeding at a bird table in a 10 minute period three times during a day. Repeat this over a number of days. Do more birds feed early in the morning? How much of the time is spent feeding and how much watching and waiting?

How quickly do birds feed? Watch birds such as blackbirds in the garden, or gulls or crows in the school grounds. Count the number of times they stop to peck at the ground in a 10 minute period. Can you see if they actually catch something? If so work out the proportion that were successful.

Nest boxes

Many birds will nest in artificial boxes. Put up two or three nest boxes in different parts of the garden or school grounds. If the

Bird tables can be on a post, or hung from a branch. They should be safe from cats and cleaned regularly.

Bird feeders can be very simple, or something more elaborate.

Bag of peanuts

Half a coconut, can be filled with fat when empty

Bread and cheese scraps

Fruit and seeds

birds decide to use your box watch for them bringing nest material. How often do they bring it? Be careful not to go too close or the birds won't come near until you have gone.

When the parents start to bring food you will know that the eggs have hatched and the young are being fed. Note the date you first see them bringing food and count how many times they visit in half an hour. A week later count again. Are they feeding more frequently as the chicks grow older? Calculate how much food they are bringing daily.

Waterbirds

If you live near a reservoir or lake where it is safe to watch birds, count the number of different species of water birds once per week or month. Are more species of birds present in greater numbers in the winter months? Some birds dive to catch their food. Find a bird that is diving and count how many dives it makes in a 10 minute period. How long does each dive last? Use a stopwatch to time 10 dives for two different species. Are the average times per dive different?

Roosts

In winter several species such as starlings and gulls form large roosts each evening. Can you track down the location of the roosts from the flight lines and count the numbers of birds arriving?

Arrival dates

Make a note of when you first see one of the summer visitors. Notice how some species arrive earlier than others.

Starlings fly in large noisy flocks to their roost site.

Sand martin MARCH 28

Swift APRIL 26

Cuckoo APRIL 15

Summer visitors arrive regularly each spring.

Presenting results

Once you have made your observations you will want to display the results. You can display the number of birds seen, on the way to school for example, using bird symbols as shown below. The diagram shows the results of a walk where the middle symbol was the most common bird, for example long-tailed tit, and the least common bird was the last symbol, perhaps heron. Different colours can be used to show whether a bird was flying or perched. If you saw a lot of birds, rather than draw a symbol for each one, you can let one symbol represent 5 birds. If you saw 30 birds you will need 30/5 = 6 symbols.

You may have collected observations at a bird table and noted which food birds were eating. Draw up a table like the one shown opposite. You can display the food preferences for each species in a pie diagram. To do this you will need to calculate the observations for each type of food as a percentage of the total of all feeding observations. Greenfinches for example fed 40 times out of 90 on peanuts or 40/90 = 44.4%. To construct a pie diagram first draw a circle.

Numbers of birds seen feeding at a garden bird table in January

Species	Length cm	Maximum number
Blue tit	11	12
Great tit	13	10
Greenfinch	14	5
Coal tit	10	2
Blackbird	25	2
Robin	14	1
Fieldfare	26	3

Species	Number of feeding occasions				
	Peanuts	Biscuit	Raisins	Apples	Total
Blue tit	169	26	4	1	200
Great tit	80	10	5	5	100
Greenfinch	40	30	15	5	90
Coal tit	35	0	0	0	35
Blackbird	0	10	15	40	65
Robin	0	22	0	5	27
Fieldfare	0	0	10	37	47

▲ *A table of observations which can easily be converted into a pie diagram or a bar chart to illustrate the results.*

A count of birds can be illustrated using symbols. On the way to school a family of long-tailed tits may be the commonest bird. ▼

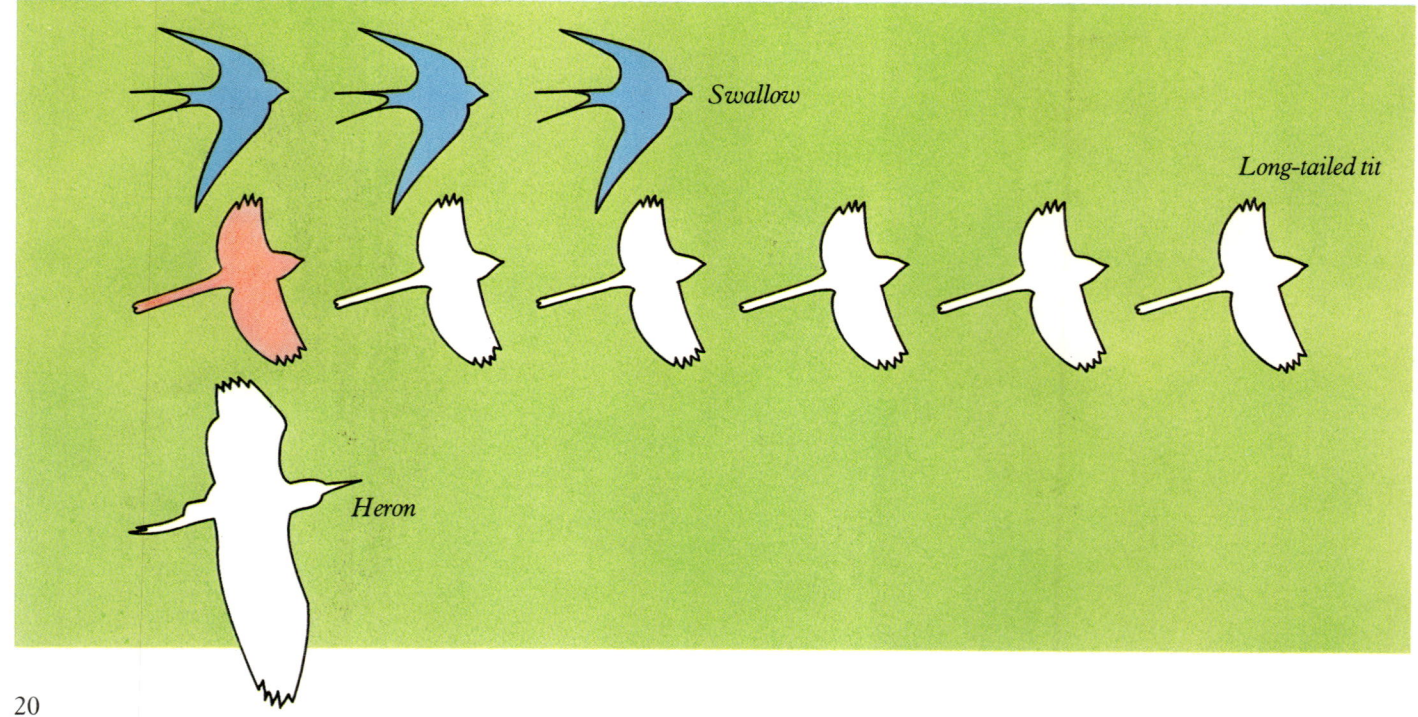

Swallow

Long-tailed tit

Heron

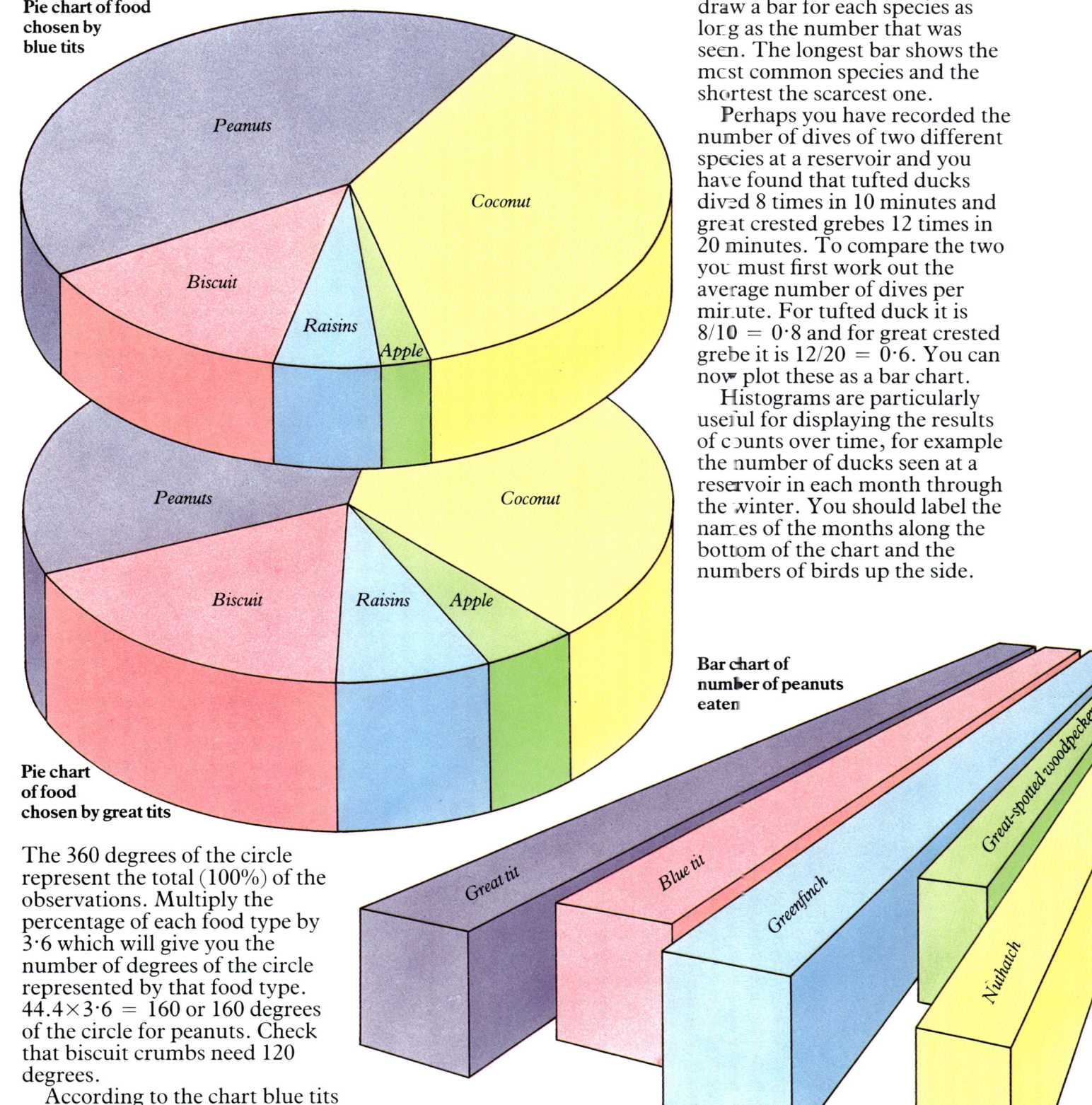

Pie chart of food chosen by blue tits

Peanuts

Coconut

Biscuit

Raisins

Apple

Pie chart of food chosen by great tits

Peanuts

Coconut

Biscuit

Raisins

Apple

Bar chart of number of peanuts eaten

Great tit

Blue tit

Greenfinch

Nuthatch

Great-spotted woodpecker

draw a bar for each species as long as the number that was seen. The longest bar shows the most common species and the shortest the scarcest one.

Perhaps you have recorded the number of dives of two different species at a reservoir and you have found that tufted ducks dived 8 times in 10 minutes and great crested grebes 12 times in 20 minutes. To compare the two you must first work out the average number of dives per minute. For tufted duck it is $8/10 = 0.8$ and for great crested grebe it is $12/20 = 0.6$. You can now plot these as a bar chart.

Histograms are particularly useful for displaying the results of counts over time, for example the number of ducks seen at a reservoir in each month through the winter. You should label the names of the months along the bottom of the chart and the numbers of birds up the side.

The 360 degrees of the circle represent the total (100%) of the observations. Multiply the percentage of each food type by 3·6 which will give you the number of degrees of the circle represented by that food type. $44.4 \times 3.6 = 160$ or 160 degrees of the circle for peanuts. Check that biscuit crumbs need 120 degrees.

According to the chart blue tits were the most common bird at the bird table. You can display the abundance of different birds using a bar chart. List the species at the side of the page, and the numbers along the bottom. Then

▲ *Two pie diagrams illustrate the amounts of food eaten by great tits and blue tits. A bar chart could be used to show how much of a particular type of food is eaten by different species.*

The computer can be put to good use presenting numerical data in a graphical way. By means of this program you can enter your own data or results, and the computer will convert them into a bar chart or pie chart. To learn how to use the program, use the data in the table on page 20. For example, you could try making charts for greenfinch food. You could make the kinds of food the headings and enter the numbers of birds trying each kind of food.

Type the program in and debug it so that it runs properly. Save the program on cassette.

```
 10 ON ERROR MODE7:END
 20 MODE7
 30 PROCINPUT
 40 REPEAT
 50    MODE7:VDU23;8202;0;0;0;
 60    PROCDATA
 70    MODE2:VDU23;8202;0;0;0;
 80    IF NH<8 THEN PROCPIE
 90    MODE1:VDU23;8202;0;0;0;
100    PROCBAR
110    UNTIL FALSE
120 END


130 DEF PROCINPUT
140 PRINT CHR$131 CHR$157 CHR$132
"         Bar/Pie Charts"
150 PRINT TAB(0,2)"    Press ESCAP
E at any time to leave        the pr
ogram."
160 INPUT TAB(0,5)"Title:"T$:T$=L
EFT$(T$,20)
170 REPEAT
180    INPUT"Number of headings:"N
H
190    UNTIL NH<25 AND NH >0
200 DIM A(3,NH),A$(NH):SUM=0:MAX=
0
210 FOR C=1 TO NH
220    PRINT CHR$134 C
230    INPUT"Heading="A$(C)"Number
="A(1,C)
240    IF A(1,C)>MAX THEN MAX=A(1,
C)
250    A$(C)=LEFT$(A$(C),10)
260    SUM=SUM+A(1,C)
270    NEXT
280 IF SUM=0 THEN RUN
290 ENDPROC
```

```
300 DEF PROCDATA
310 BL=864/MAX:UA=360/SUM
320 CLS:VDU14
330 PRINT CHR$134 T$
340 PRINT
350 FOR C=1 TO NH
360    A(2,C)=INT(A(1,C)*UA*10+.05
)/10
370    A(3,C)=A(1,C)*BL
380    PRINT;C")";A$(C):
390    PRINT"    No.=";A(1,C),"  Ang
le=";A(2,C)
400    NEXT
410 PRINT
420 PRINT CHR$134"Press SPACE BAR
to continue."
430 PROCS
440 ENDPROC


450 DEF PROCPIE
460 COLOUR135:CLS
470 COLOUR131:COLOUR0
480 PRINT TAB((20-LEN T$)/2,1)T$
490 COLOUR135
500 R=300
510 VDU29,832;636;
520 MOVE 0,R
530 A1=0
540 FOR S=1 TO NH
550    CO=S MOD7:BCO=135+7*(CO=3)
560    GCOL0,CO
570    A2=A1+A(2,S)*PI/180
580    FOR A=A1 TO A2 STEP PI/32
590       MOVE 0,0
600       PLOT 85,R*SIN A,R*COS A
610       NEXT
620    MOVE 0,0:PLOT 85,R*SIN A2,R
*COS A2
630    GCOL0,0
640    MOVE R*SIN A1,R*COS A1:DRAW
0,0
650    A1=A2
660    COLOUR CO:COLOUR BCO
670    PRINT TAB(0,21+S)A$(S):PRIN
TTAB(12,21+S) STR$(A(1,S))
680    NEXT
690 DRAW 0,R
700 FOR A=0 TO 2*PI+PI/32 STEP PI
/32
```

```
 710     DRAW R*SIN A,R*COS A
 720     NEXT
 730 COLOUR0:PRINT"Press the space
bar."
 740 PRINT TAB(1,11)"Total"
 750 COLOUR1:PRINT TAB(2,13);SUM
 760 PROCS
 770 ENDPROC


 780 DEF PROCBAR
 790 VDU19,2,2,0,0,0
 800 PRINT TAB((39-LENT$)/2,1)T$
 810 VDU5
 820 BW=704/NH
 830 MOVE0,895
 840 FOR C=1 TO NH
 850     GCOL0,1+C MOD 3
 860     PRINT A$(C)
 870     PLOT0,351,35
 880     PLOT0,A(3,C),0:PLOT81,0,-BW
 890     PLOT0,-A(3,C),BW:PLOT81,0,-
BW
 900     PLOT0,-351,0
 910     NEXT
 920 P=-1
 930 REPEAT
 940     P=P+1:PO=10^P:D=MAX/PO
 950     UNTIL D<10
 960 D=INT D
 970 GCOL0,3
 980 FOR C=-1 TO D+1
 990     MOVE351+BL*PO*C,175
1000     PLOT1,BL*PO,0:PLOT1,0,-32
1010     PLOT0,-16,-16
1020     PRINT;C+1
1030     NEXT
1040 VDU4
1050 COLOUR1:COLOUR131
1060 PRINT TAB(1,28)" *";PO;" "
1070 PRINT TAB(4,30)" Press the SP
ACE BAR to continue. "
1080 PROCS
1090 ENDPROC


1100 DEF PROCS
1110 *FX15,0
1120 REPEAT:UNTIL GET=32:ENDPROC
```

Using the program

1. Run the program.

2. Enter the title of the data. The title should not be more than 20 characters including spaces between words. Press RETURN.

3. Enter the number of headings. The maximum number is twenty-four. Press RETURN.

4. Enter the name of the first heading. Enter the number of items under that heading. Do the same for each heading in turn. Press RETURN *each time you enter an item of data.*

5. All the data with the corresponding angles for the pie chart sectors will be displayed. If you have more than 10 headings, press SHIFT *to see all the data. You can use the angles to draw the pie chart on paper. If you have less than 7 headings the computer will draw the pie chart for you. Press the* SPACE BAR.

6. The data will be displayed as a bar chart. The scale along the bottom is always 0, 1, 2, . . . Look at the white box in the bottom left-hand corner. It shows a ★ followed by a number. You must multiply the numbers on the scale by the number following the star to get the real value of the scale. Press the SPACE BAR.

7. The screen displays the data again. Press the SPACE BAR *again and the screen displays the pie chart, and so on, in a loop.*

8. Press ESCAPE *to leave the program.*

Life cycle

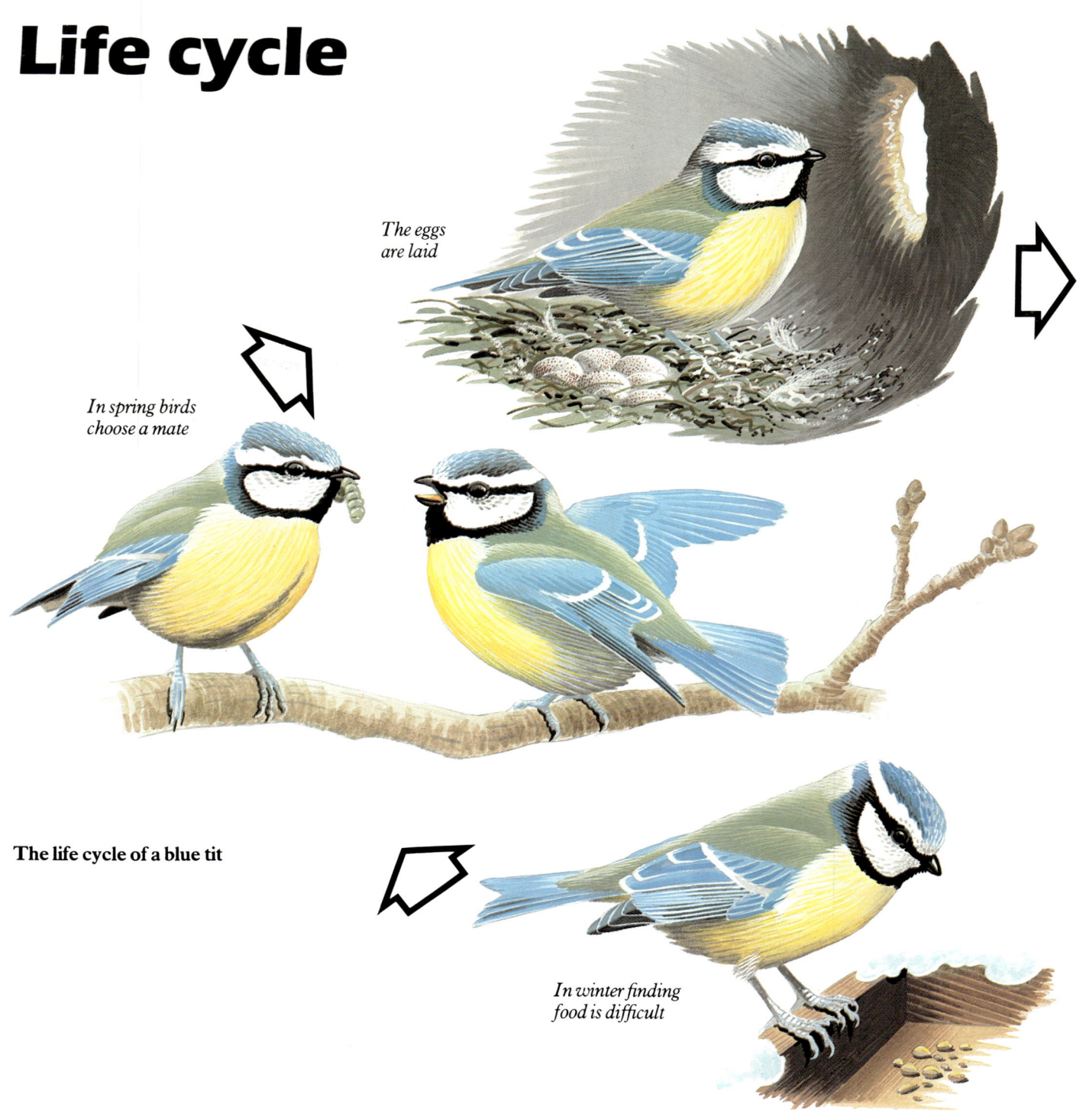

The eggs
are laid

In spring birds
choose a mate

The life cycle of a blue tit

In winter finding
food is difficult

The life of a bird is a very busy one and most of it is taken up with finding food, either for itself or its family. Most garden birds do not live long. The robin or blackbird rarely live for more than a few years. Seabirds are longer lived and some reach the age of thirty. The low life expectancy of garden birds is mainly due to the pressures of predation and climate that ensure that only the fittest survive.

At the end of the winter, birds begin to establish territories and find mates, filling the air with their songs. Once they have paired up, a nest site is sought and a nest built. Courtship continues and eventually results

▲ *After courtship the nest is built and the eggs laid. The young are reared and eventually leave the nest. Some may be taken by a predator, others become independent. Food at bird tables may help them to survive the winter until the new breeding season.*

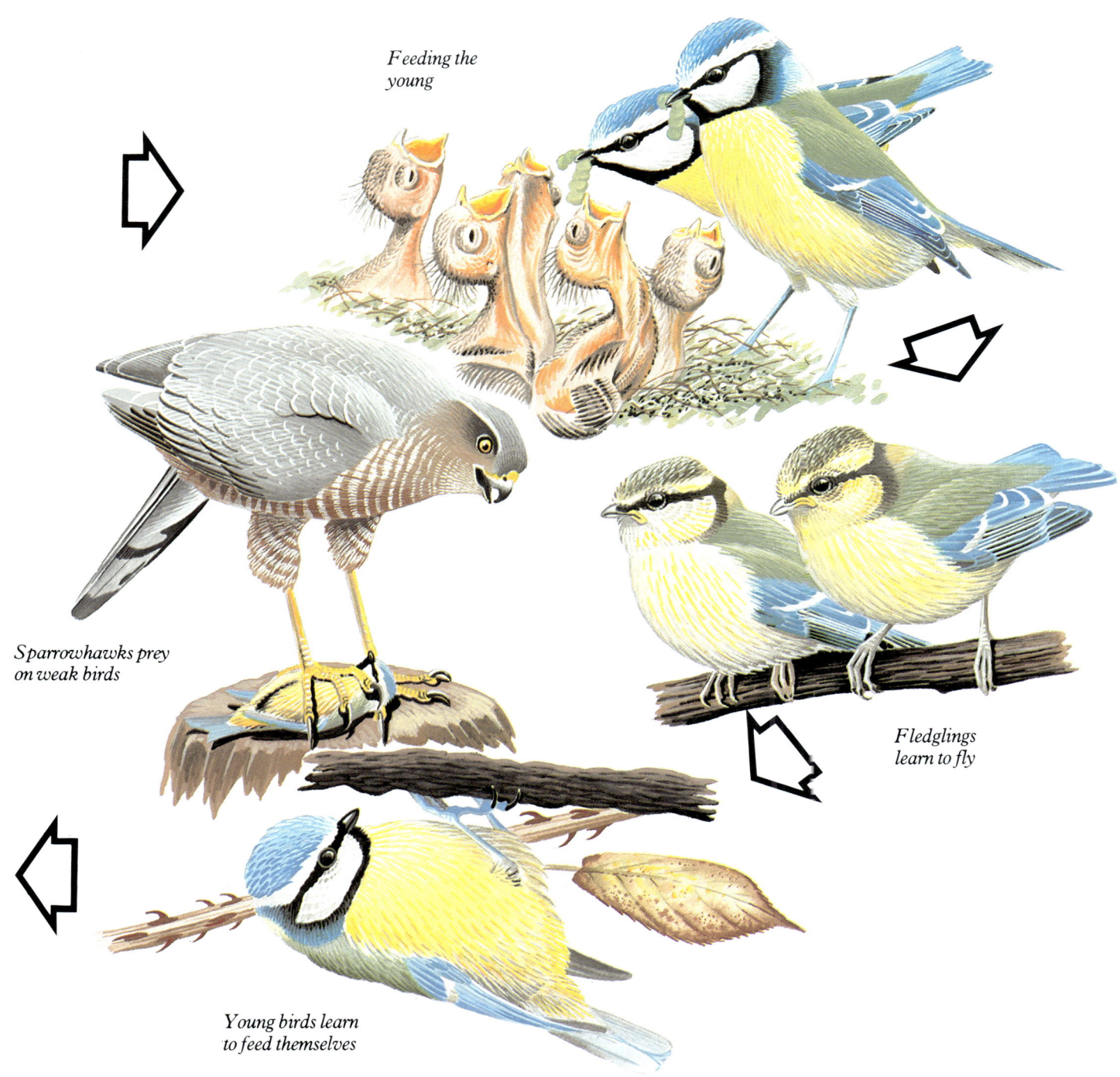

Feeding the young

Sparrowhawks prey on weak birds

Fledglings learn to fly

Young birds learn to feed themselves

in mating followed by egg laying. From this time on the nest is at risk from predators which may steal the eggs, or the nestlings.

Incubation takes a few weeks and may be shared between parents in some species. The hatching of the young usually coincides with an abundance of food. For a few weeks the

parents will have to feed the young continually and their activity makes the nest easier to find for predators. The young are at their most vulnerable at this time.

The young will eventually leave the nest and will be tended by their parents for a few weeks before gaining their independence.

Weak or foolish young will not last long. The next problem most birds face is surviving the winter which some do by migrating while others stay. Food shortages and cold temperatures will remove the last of the weaker garden birds and only the strongest survive through to next year.

Nesting preparations

◀ *Many birds have elaborate courtship displays. The gannet 'fences' with its bill to establish a bond between it and its mate.*

As spring approaches, birds begin to prepare for the breeding season. The gradual increase in daylight length triggers off changes in the birds' behaviour and appearance.

Plumage

Birds which have a different winter plumage will start to moult out of it, some changing their colours completely, others simply becoming brighter. Ptarmigans are all white in winter to blend in against a snowy background and in spring they moult into a grey plumage to match the rocks which become exposed. Black-headed gulls, which have white heads in winter, acquire dark chocolate coloured head feathers for breeding. Even male house sparrows become brighter with a larger black bib.

Diet

Some birds will change their diet as the weather gets warmer and insects become more abundant. Blackbirds and song thrushes, which have survived the winter by feeding on fruit can now feed on worms again. Great spotted woodpeckers look for grubs instead of nuts. The presence of insects also heralds the arrival of summer visitors. All birds must be well fed and healthy before they begin the strenuous breeding season.

Territories

Some birds remain close to their home territory throughout the year while others will be forced to move further afield in their search for sufficient food for the winter. Many of our breeding birds migrate to Africa to find insect food in winter and each spring they return here to re-establish their territories.

The male bird first selects an area of suitable habitat that contains likely nest sites and that is sufficiently large to contain enough food for himself and his prospective family. He then declares that it is his by singing prominently and fending off any intruding males. Mistle thrushes sing from the tops of trees, skylarks hover high in the sky in song and woodpeckers drum against tree trunks.

Song also performs another function in attracting a female to a male's territory. When a female appears the male will display to attract her further. These displays may involve coloured plumage, ornate feathers and special calls all of which are incorporated in elaborate courtship movements.

Mapping territories

Territories can be studied by observing the song posts of birds. Choose a common bird like a robin or song thrush whose song you can recognise. Mark out on a map an area to visit and note down on it where any birds are singing. On subsequent visits mark down the song posts again and eventually a cluster of marks will appear within each territory. Draw a line around the marks and this will give you an idea of the territory size. Two birds fighting might indicate the boundary of a territory. A similar study can be done marking different species on the same map and this will give you a rough idea of how many birds can use the same area.

Song posts indicate likely territories

Goldcrest sings in yew

Mistle thrush sings at the top of a tall tree

Skylark sings above farmland

Great spotted woodpecker drums in woodland

Willow warbler sings in woodland

Chaffinch sings in woodland

Yellowhammer sings in a hawthorn hedge

Wren sings in garden bushes

Breeding

Nests

When a male has attracted a female they begin to look for a suitable nest site, which in some cases will have already been found by the male. A good nest site must be well protected from predators such as weasels, rats, cats, crows and humans. Some birds nest in close proximity to humans: house sparrows, starlings and swifts will nest in roof spaces; jackdaws in chimneys; house martins under eaves; and robins and swallows in outhouses.

Some tits, nuthatches and woodpeckers use tree cavities, often enlarging existing holes to make an appropriately sized chamber. Owls and some ducks will also use existing tree holes whilst blue and great tits readily use nest boxes. Birds which nest on the ground must have well protected nests. Wheatears nest in burrows, some warblers and pipits nest in dense tussocks of grass, whilst lapwings have nests out in the open but eggs which are well camouflaged.

A variety of nesting materials are used: house martins build their nests of mud; long-tailed tits used spider's webs, lichen and feathers; blue tits use mainly moss; and rooks use bare sticks. Nests are often found lined with soft materials like hair, wool, feathers, moss or fine grass.

Nests vary in their structure. Blackbirds have open nests with a central cup, and long-tailed tits have an enclosed nest with a side opening. The nests of many ground nesting birds, like waders, are no more than a

Rook's nest

Long tailed tit's nest

Willow warbler's nest

House martin's nest

▲ *Rooks use bare sticks for making nests, long-tailed tits use lichen and feathers, willow warblers use grass and house martins use mud.*

◄ *Guillemots are seabirds which nest on cliffs in large colonies. These ledges are also shared by kittiwakes and shags.*

◀ A starling brings a beakful of insects to its nest and is met by the bright gapes of its hungry young.

Young

Eggs are incubated by one or both parents, most garden birds taking about two weeks to hatch, larger birds a little longer. Some newly hatched young have feathers and can run or fly after a few days, others are naked and helpless, needing constant care for two to three weeks. Regular food is important and a lot is needed for the young to develop their feathers and leave the nest.

Cuckoos differ in their breeding habits as they lay a single egg in the nest of another species and let a host bird rear their young. On hatching the young cuckoo will push out any other young or eggs in the host bird's nest so it alone is tended. A young cuckoo grows to be several times larger than the bird feeding it.

After leaving the nest many birds are still cared for by their parents for a few weeks. At this stage they are highly vulnerable and many die. Eventually they gain their independence by learning to feed themselves. If they survive either a long return migration flight or a cold winter they will live to the next breeding season.

shallow unlined scrape. Nests also vary from small and neat to large and untidy.

Nest building is usually performed by both birds although the male may only help to collect material. Male wrens build a number of nests and one is chosen by the female who finishes the nest by lining it. Old nests from a previous year or brood can be repaired and used again, and some birds use a traditional nest site for years, but this is rare.

Eggs

Once the nest has been built the birds mate and the eggs are laid. Some seabirds, like guillemots lay only one egg, pigeons lay two and most small birds lay four to seven eggs, at about daily intervals. Some birds will have more than one brood each season, while others, like blue tits have only one brood which numbers nine to eleven. The eggs are protected for most of the time by the incubating parent; any eggs which are left exposed could be predated. Ground nesting birds are particularly vulnerable and may try to lead a predator away by feigning injury. Their eggs are always patterned to blend in with their surroundings. Hole nesting birds tend to lay white eggs.

Program: COLONY

This program is a simulation of the development of a guillemot colony. Like all simulations it presents only an approximation of reality. It will help you to understand how different factors can influence the growth of a seabird colony.

Type the program in and debug it so that it runs properly. Save the program on cassette.

```
 10 ON ERROR MODE7:END
 20 MODE7
 30 PROCSTART
 40 REPEAT
 50   MODE1:VDU23;8202;0;0;0;
 60   VDU24,0;255;1279;1023;
 70   VDU19,2,4,0,0,0
 80   COLOUR130:CLS
 90   GCOL0,129:CLG
100   PROCFACTORS
110   PROCGRAPH
120   *FX15,0
130   REPEAT:UNTIL GET=32
140   UNTIL FALSE
150 END


160 DEF PROCSTART
170 PRINT TAB(4,3)CHR$134"COLONY
SIMULATION"
180 PRINT
190 INPUT"Colony start size (betw
een 50 and 800) ? "SIZE
200 IF SIZE<50 OR SIZE>800 THEN P
RINT CHR$129"Out of range !":GOTO19
0
210 PRINT
220 INPUT"How many years (from 10
to 120) ? "YEARS
230 IF YEARS<10 OR YEARS>120 THEN
 PRINT CHR$129"Out of range !":GOTO
220
240 PRINT
250 PRINT"Max. colony size (from
";STR$(SIZE);" to 800) ";:INPUT MAX
260 IF MAX>800 OR MAX<SIZE THEN P
RINT CHR$129 "Out of range !":GOTO2
50
270 ENDPROC
```

```
280 DEF PROCFACTORS
290 F$=" factor: R H L S ?"
300 PRINT TAB(0,26)"Colony "F$
310 I$=GET$:IF INSTR("RHLS",I$)=0
THEN280
320 PRINT TAB(16,26)I$"        "
330 IR=.68:IL=.66
340 IF I$="L" OR I$="H" THEN IR=I
R/2
350 IF I$="H" THEN IL=IL+IR
360 IF I$="S" THEN IR=0:REPEAT:IL
=VAL GET$:UNTIL IL>0:PRINT TAB(17,2
6);IL:IL=IL-1:IL=.66+.68*IL/8
370 PRINT TAB(0,28)"Weather"F$
380 J$=GET$:IF INSTR("RHLS",J$)=0
THEN340
390 PRINT TAB(16,28)J$"        "
400 JR=1.5:JL=.25
410 IF J$="L" OR J$="H" THEN JR=J
R/2
420 IF J$="H" THEN JL=JL+JR
430 IF J$="S" THEN JR=0:REPEAT:JL
=VAL GET$:UNTIL JL>0:PRINT TAB(17,2
8);JL:JL=JL-1:JL=.25+1.5*JL/8
440 PRINT TAB(0,30)"Oiling "F$
450 K$=GET$:IF INSTR("RHLS",K$)=0
THEN410
460 PRINT TAB(16,30)K$"        "
470 KR=1:KL=.5
480 IF K$="L" OR K$="H" THEN KR=K
R/2
490 IF K$="H" THEN KL=KL+KR
500 IF K$="S" THEN KR=0:REPEAT:KL
=VAL GET$:UNTIL KL>0:PRINT TAB(17,3
0);KL:KL=KL-1:KL=.5+KL/8
510 LEAVERS=0
520 ADULTS=SIZE:AGE1=SIZE*.175:AG
E2=SIZE*.125:AGE3=SIZE*.1
530 ENDPROC


540 DEF PROCGRAPH
550 HF=600/MAX
560 W=INT(960/YEARS)
570 GCOL0,0
580 MOVE 151,967:DRAW 151,327:DRA
W 1151,327
590 MOVE 151,935:PLOT 1,-32,0
600 MOVE W*YEARS+159,327:PLOT 1,0
,-32
610 GCOL0,3
```

```
  620 PRINT TAB(0,2)STR$(MAX)TAB(0,
8)"Pop."
  630 PRINT TAB(17,22)"Years"TAB(34
,23)STR$(YEARS)
  640 MOVE 159,335
  650 VDU28,21,30,38,25:COLOUR131:C
LS
  660 COLOUR2
  670 FOR N=0 TO YEARS-1:PROCNEWYEA
R:H=SIZE*HF
  680   PRINT TAB(1,1)"Colony size
";SIZE;"    "
  690   IF SIZE=0 THEN N=YEARS-1
  700   PLOT 1,0,H:PLOT 81,W,0:PLOT
 1,0,-H:PLOT 81,-W,0:PLOT 1,W,0
  710   NEXT
  720 PRINT TAB(1,3)"Leavers ";LEAV
ERS
  730 ENDPROC



  740 DEF PROCNEWYEAR
  750 I=RND(1)*IR+IL:J=RND(1)*JR+JL
:K=RND(1)*KR+KL

  760 REM First eggs laid by mid Ma
y,              one egg per pair of
adults.
  770 EGGS=INT(ADULTS/2)

  780 REM Chicks hatch mid June.
  790 CHICKS=EGGS-.2*EGGS*I

  800 REM Both parents and young le
ave            cliffs by end of July.
  810 YOUNGBIRDS=CHICKS-CHICKS*(.08
75+.0375*I)

  820 REM Guillemots do not breed u
ntil           their fourth year.
  830 NEWADULTS=AGE3-AGE3*(.05*K+.0
5*(.5+J/2))

  840 AGE3=AGE2-AGE2*(.04*K+.16*(.5
+J/2))
  850 AGE2=AGE1-AGE1*(.057*K+.229*J
)
  860 REM Young birds have to survi
ve             the winter months.
  870 AGE1=YOUNGBIRDS-YOUNGBIRDS*(.
057*K+.4*J+.043)
```

```
  880 REM Some of the original adul
ts             die too.
  890 ADULTS=ADULTS+NEWADULTS-ADULT
S*(.025*K+.055*(.5+J/2))

  900 SIZE=INT ADULTS
  910 D=MAX-SIZE
  920 IF D>=0 THEN ENDPROC
  930 ADULTS=ADULTS+D:LEAVERS=LEAVE
RS-D
  940 SIZE=INT ADULTS
  950 ENDPROC
```

How to use the program
1. Run the program.

2. Enter the number of birds in the colony to start with (colony start size), the number of years for which you want the simulation to run, and the maximum number of birds the colony can support.

3. There are three factors which influence the development of the colony. The first is called the colony factor. This includes predation, accidental damage to eggs, and so on. Choose whether you want the colony factor to be completely random (press R), high/random (press H), low/random (press L), or whether you want to set the colony factor at a fixed value (press S followed by any number from 1 to 9).
Now do the same for the weather and oiling factors. On the screen you will see a graph of how the number of adult birds (population) changes over the years. If the colony grows to more than your maximum size then the extra birds will leave. Leavers shows how many left the colony during the time period.

4. Press the SPACE BAR. You can now choose the values for the three factors again. The graph will be drawn again using the same number of years and the same maximum colony size, but the start size will be the number of adult birds left after the previous time span.

5. Press ESCAPE and type RUN if you want to start again with a new colony.

Migration

When autumn approaches many birds will have difficulty in finding food. Daylight decreases, temperatures fall and as a result many insects become scarce. These changes in climate affect summer visitors which prepare to migrate. Warblers, flycatchers, cuckoos, swallows and martins are unable to survive northern winters and so most of them fly south to Africa where the climate is warmer and food more plentiful. An estimated 5,000 million birds migrate from Europe and Asia into Africa each autumn.

As summer visitors are preparing to leave, other birds which breed much further north in Greenland, Iceland, Scandinavia and Siberia are doing likewise. They also move south and many of these will spend their winter in the milder parts of Europe. Millions of ducks, geese and swans as well as thrushes, like fieldfares and redwings, finches, like bramblings and siskins, and even familiar species arrive each autumn to join the resident birds. Some of the starlings, blackbirds and robins that you feed in the winter could easily have come from Finland or Russia.

Each spring a reverse movement occurs. The birds return in their bright breeding plumage but always fewer than departed.

It is difficult to believe that a small bird like a swallow is able to find its way to South Africa and back to Europe each year,

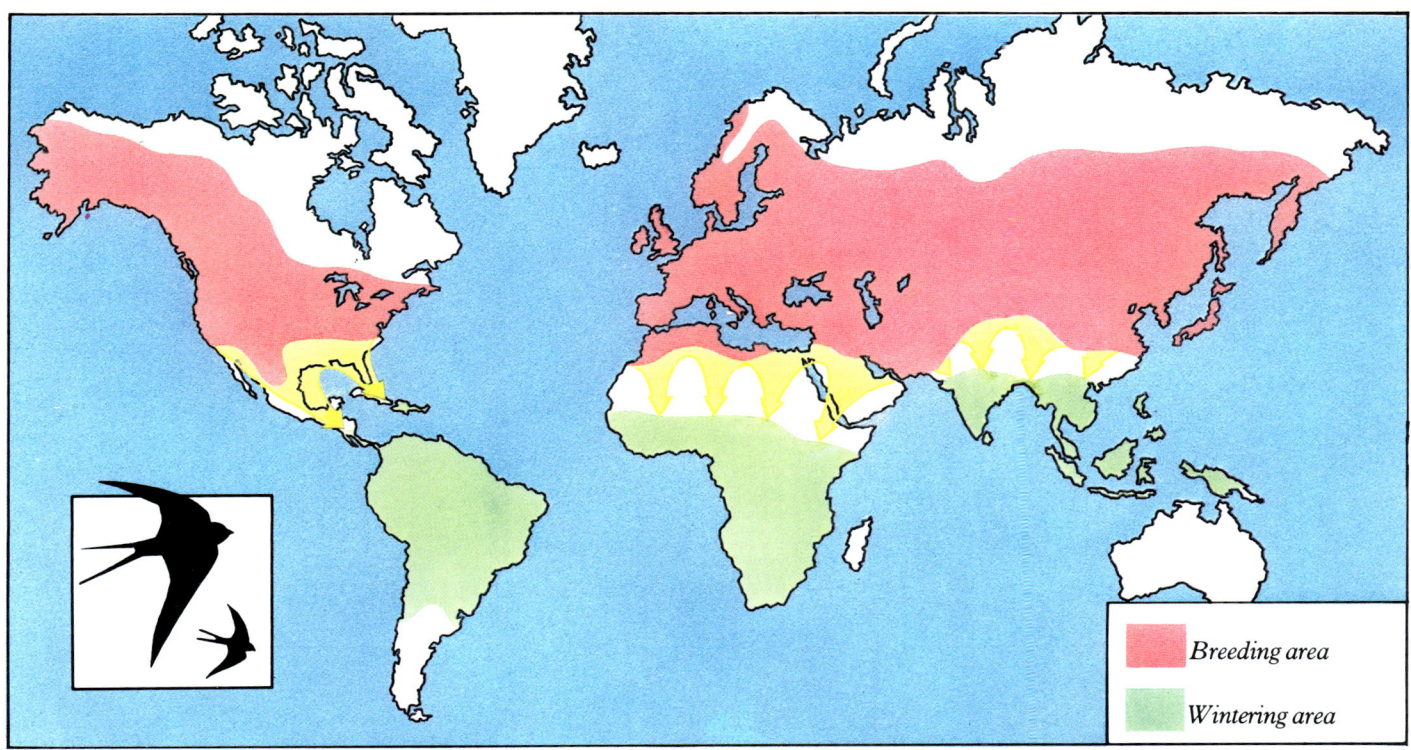

▲ *The swallow breeds in Europe, North America, and Asia, migrating south to Africa, South America and south-east Asia each winter.*

Barnacle geese breed in Greenland, Spitzbergen, and Siberia. Each population migrates to a different wintering area. ▶

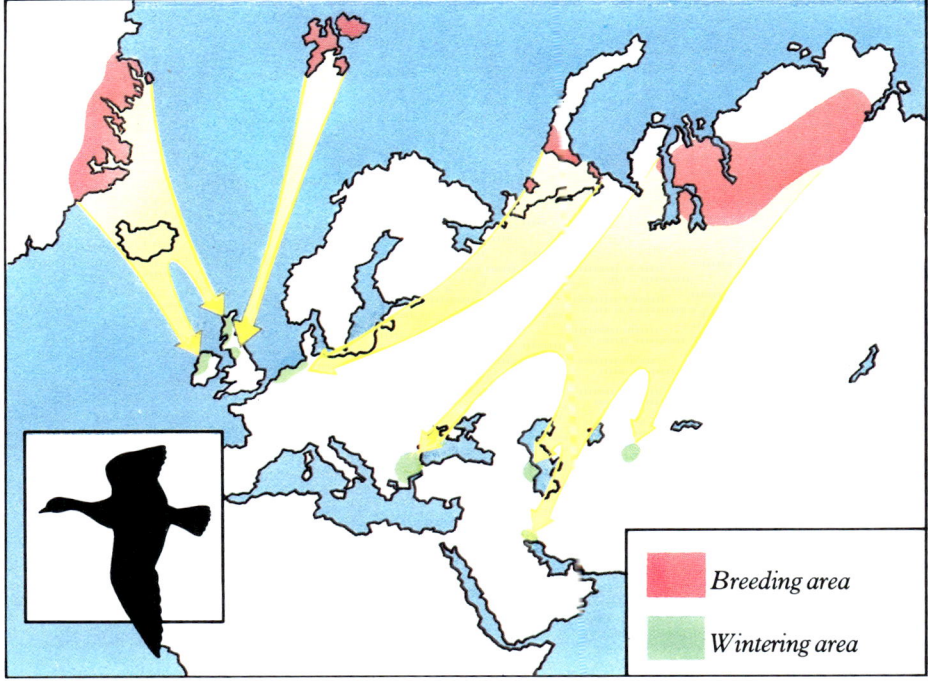

returning to the same area, sometimes to the same building where it was born. The oldest recorded British swallow was 16 years old and must have flown an incredible 320,000 km in its lifetime.

How do birds do it? The answer is unclear. We know that they are able to navigate using both the sun and the stars. Some can detect the earth's magnetic field and variations in gravity may also help them to find their way. As they near their journey's end they probably use landmarks to take them back to their old nest sites.

Preparing for migration is very important. Migrants spend a great deal of time feeding before setting off and they will be substantially heavier than normal when they leave. Some species fly the distance in one go, others take it in stages, stopping to feed as they progress. The routes taken by European birds as they migrate differ. Some will fly south straight over the Sahara while many others will skirt around it by flying along the west African coast. Many will fly along the eastern Mediterranean coast and enter Africa through Egypt.

Similar migration patterns are found between eastern Asia and Australasia, and North and South America.

The use of a database to record birds feeding at a bird table is described on page 17. Many other observations can be recorded using a database; counts of birds anywhere: a walk to school, a visit to a local reservoir, a list of birds seen in a week, month, or year, including details where they were seen or what the habitat was. Remember that it is important to make your entries under each heading consistent. If you describe one species as found in woods and another in woodland, this will register as two different entries as if they were different habitats.

Migration database

On the pages opposite you will find a table of information about migrating birds. Try storing this on a database and then answering the following questions.

Which bird travels furthest?

How many birds spend the winter in west Africa?

Where do insect eaters migrate to?

Which species live for more than 15 years?

Which is the lightest bird to fly over 5,000 km?

▼ *A database program is used to store information which can then be retrieved and related.*

Hints on setting up the database

You will need to make your categories or headings the same as the headings in the table. You may find that the database you are using has a limit to the number of letters that can be included in the heading. If this happens you will have to use an abbreviated heading. For example if your headings are limited to six letters 'wingspan' could be entered as 'wgspan' or 'wingsp'. You must always be careful to use the same abbreviation for the headings. Likewise, when you make a descriptive entry under a heading, the same word must be used for the same description. For example under the heading 'main food' the computer will not recognize that fish and fishes are the same food item and will treat them separately.

When you are entering data into the database always check that you have typed everything correctly. Spelling mistakes can mean that the information is stored in the wrong place and it will be difficult to retrieve it.

If you are preparing a table of your own information it is helpful to write out the data on squared paper. You can then see if any of the headings need to be modified or abbreviated to fit. Try this with the migration table. If you need to stop work on your database before you have finished entering it, remember to store what you have done on a cassette and then you can come back to complete it later. Any file should be clearly labelled on the cassette and if you want to ensure that it is not erased, the plastic tabs should be broken off the edge of the cassette. Sticky tape placed over the holes will enable you to record on the cassette later should you wish to.

Migration Table

This table illustrates the general breeding and wintering areas of a selection of migrants.
The distance travelled is also only approximate.

Species	Breeding area	Wintering area	Distance travelled km	Weight g	Wing span cm	Oldest known	Main food
Manx shearwater	Europe	S America	12,000	450	85	30	Fish
Gannet	Europe	W Africa	5,300	3,000	175	25	Fish
Garganey	Europe	Africa	4,500	340	62	6	Vegetation
Pintail	Siberia	Europe	5,500	800	88	17	Vegetation
Bewick's swan	Siberia	Europe	4,500	6,000	190	19	Vegetation
Barnacle goose	Spitzbergen	Europe	2,700	1,800	140	20	Vegetation
Osprey	Europe	W Africa	5,000	1,500	152	13	Fish
Knot	Siberia	Europe	7,500	152	59	16	Invertebrates
Sanderling	Greenland	Europe	2,500	57	42	13	Invertebrates
Dunlin	Siberia	Europe	4,600	47	40	15	Invertebrates
Common sandpiper	Europe	E Africa	4,700	57	40	9	Invertebrates
Sandwich tern	Europe	S Africa	10,400	242	94	21	Fish
Arctic tern	Europe	Antarctica	18,000	94	79	27	Fish
Cuckoo	Europe	Africa	5,400	114	60	9	Insects
Swift	Europe	S Africa	9,800	39	40	16	Insects
Swallow	Europe	S Africa	10,400	19	34	16	Insects
House martin	Europe	C Africa	4,700	18	31	6	Insects
Tree pipit	Europe	Africa	4,500	22	28	6	Insects
Yellow wagtail	Europe	E Africa	4,800	17	26	7	Insects
Redstart	Europe	Africa	5,000	15	25	8	Insects
Wheatear	Greenland	Africa	7,000	26	30	7	Insects
Redwing	N Russia	Europe	4,000	65	36	7	Invertebrates
Sedge warbler	Europe	Africa	5,000	11	20	6	Insects
Blackcap	Europe	Africa	4,800	17	23	7	Insects
Willow warbler	Europe	Africa	5,300	8	21	7	Insects
Goldcrest	N Europe	Europe	1,300	6	16	5	Insects
Spotted flycatcher	Europe	S Africa	10,000	15	26	9	Insects
Pied flycatcher	Europe	W Africa	5,000	13	24	7	Insects
Brambling	N Russia	Europe	3,200	24	27	7	Seeds

Habitats

Habitat describes the area in which a bird lives. Usually habitats differ from each other most noticeably in the amount and type of vegetation. Gardens with lawns, hedges, shrubs and few trees are an example of a habitat. This habitat is probably the one with which you are most familiar. There are many different habitats. They can be divided into three main groups below: those with many trees, those with few, and areas of water.

Different habitats	
Woodland	*Broadleaved and coniferous*
Open country	*Farmland with hedges and without hedges*
	Heathlands
	Moorlands
	Mountains
	Gardens
	Parkland
	Towns and cities
Water	*Marshes and fens*
	Lakes, ponds, reservoirs and flooded gravel pits
	Fast and slow flowing rivers, and canals
	Beaches
	Estuaries
	Rocks and cliffs

Some birds, such as the wren, are found in many different habitats. Others are more specialized and only found in one or two, for example the guillemot which only breeds on sea cliffs. Pick two or three different habitats from the list, for example gardens, woods and lakes, and spend an hour in each. Record how many species you see. Then use the computer to draw a bar chart of the numbers of different species in each habitat. You can compare the numbers of birds in the natural broadleaved with planted coniferous woodland, or birds at a natural lake with those at an artificial reservoir.

Notice that where a species occurs in all habitats numbers are often different. If you are able to visit a completely different habitat such as the seashore, make counts of the birds you see. Compare these counts with counts you made at home or with those made by friends.

The numbers of species in each habitat also change with the seasons. For example if you make counts of birds at reservoirs you will often find that numbers of ducks are highest in winter. If on the other hand, you make counts of other birds around the edge of the water, you will find that these are highest in the summer. Estuaries are particularly interesting. In the winter there are often many thousands of waders and ducks. In summer there are fewer species and many fewer birds. When you have read the migration section you should be able to say why.

◄ *Herons feed on fish and other aquatic animals and are usually found near water.*

Many birds are restricted to one sort of habitat. To see a good variety you should visit all of the different habitats near you. ►

Mountains

Moorlands

Marshland

Heathlands

Farmland

Gardens

Rocks and
cliffs

This program is a game in which you must match the bird to its habitat. The different habitats appear as symbols. As each bird name is printed on the screen, you must choose one of the habitats for the bird. Each habitat symbol has a number next to it. Type in the number next to your chosen symbol. If you are right the habitat will colour in, and after a second a new bird name will appear. If you are wrong you must choose again.

Type the program in and debug it so that it runs properly. Save the program on cassette.

```
 10 MODE1
 20 VDU23;8202;0;0;0;
 30 PROCUDG
 40 PROCDISPLAY
 50 REPEAT
 60   PROCSELECT
 70   PROCANSWER
 80   UNTIL FALSE
 90 END


100 DEFPROCUDG
110 REM Farmland
120 VDU23,224,0,0,12,8,8,8,63,63
130 VDU23,225,0,0,0,0,0,2,226,254
140 VDU23,226,63,63,63,24,60,60,24,0
150 VDU23,227,248,188,126,126,126,126,
60,0
160 REM Reedbeds
170 VDU23,228,0,0,8,8,42,42,42,42
180 VDU23,229,0,8,8,8,40,40,40,40
190 VDU23,230,42,42,127,127,127,127,12
7,0
200 VDU23,231,40,40,254,254,254,254,25
4,0
210 REM Sea cliffs and rocky shores
220 VDU23,232,0,64,64,96,96,96,96,112
230 VDU23,233,0,0,0,0,0,0,0,0
240 VDU23,234,112,112,112,120,124,127,
127,0
250 VDU23,235,0,0,0,64,240,254,254,0
260 REM Mooorlands and mountains
270 VDU23,236,0,8,12,12,30,30,31,63
280 VDU23,237,0,0,8,8,28,60,62,254
290 VDU23,238,63,63,127,127,127,127,12
7,0
```

```
300 VDU23,239,254,254,254,254,254,254,
254,0
310 REM Woodlands (broadleaved)
320 VDU23,240,0,7,15,31,31,63,63,31
330 VDU23,241,0,0,192,224,240,240,240,
224
340 VDU23,242,7,3,3,3,3,7,127,0
350 VDU23,243,192,0,0,0,0,128,254,0
360 REM Lakes and reservoirs
370 VDU23,244,0,0,0,0,0,0,64,64
380 VDU23,245,0,0,0,0,0,0,0,0
390 VDU23,246,96,96,112,127,127,127,12
7,0
400 VDU23,247,2,2,6,254,254,254,254,0
410 ENDPROC


420 DEFPROCBOX(C,D,N)
430 COLOUR C:FOR A=0TO3:PRINT TAB(3+N*
3/2,A+6)"    ":NEXT
440 COLOUR131:COLOUR D:PRINT TAB(4+N*3
/2,7);:VDU224+N,225+N,10,8,8,226+N,227+N
450 COLOUR1:PRINT TAB(4+N*3/2,11);N/4+
1
460 ENDPROC


470 DEFPROCDISPLAY
480 VDU19,0,4,0,0,0:COLOUR131:COLOUR1:
CLS
490 PRINT TAB(9,2)"***   Habitat Game
***"
500 C=128:D=0
510 FOR N=0TO20 STEP4:PROCBOX(C,D,N):N
EXT
520 COLOUR0
530 FOR N=1 TO6:RESTORE(780+N*10):READ
H$:PRINT TAB(4,22+N)STR$(N);". ";H$:NEXT
540 COLOUR1
550 ENDPROC


560 DEFPROCSELECT
570 H=RND(6):R=RND(8)
580 RESTORE(780+H*10)
590 READH$,C,D
600 FOR N=1 TO R:READ B$:NEXT
610 PRINT TAB(7,15)STRING$(200," ")
620 TIME=0:REPEAT:UNTIL TIME=100
630 COLOUR0:PRINT TAB(7,15)"Where do y
ou think a" TAB(7,19)"lives ?"
640 COLOUR1:PRINT TAB(7,17)B$
650 ENDPROC
```

```
 660  DEFPROCANSWER
 670  *FX15,0
 680  A$=GET$:IF A$="" THEN 680
 690  IF A$<>STR$(H) THEN SOUND1,-12,0,5
:GOTO 680
 700  FOR S=60 TO 104 STEP4:SOUND1,-12,S
,1:NEXT
 710  VDU19,1,C,0,0,0,19,2,D,0,0,0
 720  PROCBOX(129,2,(H-1)*4)
 730  FOR P=1TO8000:NEXT
 740  VDU19,1,1,0,0,0,19,2,4,0,0,0
 750  PROCBOX(128,0,(H-1)*4)
 760  COLOUR1:COLOUR131
 770  ENDPROC


 780  REM Birds
 790  DATA Farmland,2,1,yellowhammer,lin
net,red legged partridge,grey partridge,
kestrel,little owl,lapwing,skylark
 800  DATA Reedbeds,6,2,bearded tit,mars
h harrier,bittern,reed warbler,water rai
l,sedge warbler,reed bunting,Cetti´s war
bler
 810  DATA Sea cliffs & rocky shores,6,4
,guillemot,razorbill,shag,kittiwake,fulm
ar,gannet,rock pipit,puffin
 820  DATA Moorlands and mountains,5,0,g
olden eagle,ptarmigan,red grouse,ring ou
zel,dotterel,golden plover,wheatear,merl
in
 830  DATA Woodlands (broadleaved),1,2,g
reat spotted woodpecker,nuthatch,sparrow
hawk,wood warbler,pied flycatcher,hawfin
ch,woodcock,treecreeper
 840  DATA Lakes and reservoirs,5,6,mall
ard,tufted duck,great crested grebe,mute
 swan,coot,pochard,kingfisher,common san
dpiper,
```

About this program

1. Lines 10–80 are the control routine for the program. They call up the various procedures as required.

2. Lines 100–410 are PROCUDG. These lines create the user defined graphics which produce the habitat symbols. Each symbol is made up of four user defined graphics printed in a block.

3. Lines 420–460 are PROCBOX. This procedure draws the symbols and also draws a box around the symbol. It uses the variables C, D, and N. C = box colour, D = symbol colour, N = position of the symbol across the screen.

4. Lines 780–840 contain the bird name and habitat data. Each line has a habitat name followed by a box colour number, a habitat symbol colour number and a list of birds' names.

Design your own symbols

You could redesign the symbols used in this program, or define your own for use in another program. The following method can be used for modes 0, 1, 2, 4 or 5.

1. Design your symbol on squared paper using an 8 by 8 square. Here is an example.

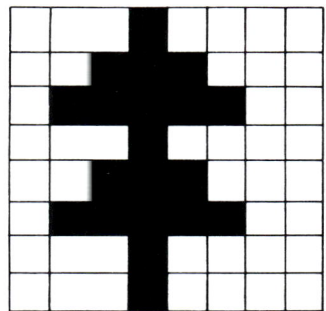

2. Turn the square into a list of binary numbers. A blank square is a 0 and a shaded square is a 1. In the example the top row is 00010000. When you have worked out each row you will have 8 binary numbers.

3. Change your binary numbers into denary numbers. You may need some help with this. You can use the chart below.

128	64	32	16	8	4	2	1	
0	0	0	1	0	0	0	0	= 16
0	0	1	1	1	0	0	0	= 32 + 16 + 8 = 56

When you have finished you will have eight denary numbers: one for each line of your graphics square.

4. To transfer your graphics to the computer you use the command VDU 23. You are allowed to design 32 symbols but each must be identified by a number from 224 to 255. For the first symbol the command begins VDU 23, 224. You must then add the eight numbers for your symbol working from the top row down. The whole command for the example is: VDU 23, 224, 16, 56, 124, 16, 56, 124, 16, 16

5. You can print your symbol on the screen by using VDU 224 or PRINT CHR$(224). You can position your symbol on the screen by using the PRINT TAB(X,Y) command. Try this program.

```
 10   MODE 5
 20   VDU 23,224,16,56,124,16.56,124,16,16
 30   PRINT TAB(9,15);CHR$(224)
```

Conservation

Nature conservation means the wise use of the natural environment to preserve and protect all forms of natural life. Birds and their habitats are a part of this. Nature conservation is probably more important today than ever before because people are rapidly destroying so much of the natural environment. Look around you and you will readily see examples: removal of hedgerows, felling of woods and draining of wet areas; pollution of rivers and marshes with rubbish and sometimes chemicals; as well as land disappearing under new motorways, houses and factories.

Probably the greatest threat to birds is the loss of their habitat. Birds depend on their individual habitat to supply them with their particular type of food. Loss of this habitat may force them into areas where this food is scarce. Many birds that breed in wetland areas are particularly at risk because of the extensive draining operations that take place to create more farmland. When this happens waders such as snipe and redshank are unable to breed in the new habitat and disappear from the site. The gorse and heather clad heaths of southern England are another habitat under threat. They are the only place in Britain where the Dartford warbler breeds. There are not many of these heaths left, yet each year more is ploughed up and the birds and other wildlife are lost.

Much natural woodland is being destroyed too. If it is not simply felled and cleared for agriculture, conifers are planted in the wood and the once deciduous wood slowly becomes

a coniferous one, an unsuitable habitat for some of the scarcer species.

Some of the scarcer breeding birds, especially waders and birds of prey, are found in upland moorlands. Many of these areas have been planted with extensive conifer forests. Although some species such as the coal tit and goldcrest survive well in such plantations the waders and birds of prey cannot. Other moorlands are gradually being turned to agriculture and again whilst some other species can live in the new habitat, the original species disappear.

Pollution

Pollution can cause problems for some birds. Oil discharged at sea from tankers and other vessels floats on the surface. Swimming or diving birds come into contact with it and often become badly

◀ *This gannet is covered in oil from a tanker. It cannot fly, swim or dive properly and is one of thousands of birds that die in this way each year.*

Protection

Birds can be protected from some of these problems by creating nature reserves which protect the habitat. With careful management by wardens the natural habitats can be maintained. Legislation also helps to protect birds by making illegal the damaging or destruction of special areas of wildlife, called Sites of Special Scientific Interest, and also making it illegal to disturb or destroy many species of birds. The nests of all birds are protected by law. Although nature reserves and legislation are helping to protect birds the best way is through education, so that people and nature can live together and the unnecessary destruction of all forms of wildlife is avoided.

oiled. Some struggle ashore alive but others, probably most, die at sea and their bodies are blown ashore by the wind. The birds most frequently oiled are those that spend most time on the sea surface, particularly razorbills and guillemots. Birds such as gulls often have oil splodges on their plumage but these rarely kill them.

In the 1960s the use of some organochlorine chemicals caused serious problems for predatory birds, particularly the heron, sparrowhawk and peregrine. These chemicals reached the birds through the food chain. Small quantitites of the chemicals in the bodies of the prey accumulated in the bodies of the predators until they eventually died of poisoning. Another effect of these chemicals was to reduce the thickness of the egg shells so that the parent birds unavoidably broke their own eggs. Fortunately the amounts of these chemicals used today have been reduced and most bird populations have recovered to their former levels.

▲ *Removing a hedge also removes associated wildlife and deprives birds of places to breed, feed and roost.*

Woodland takes a long time to grow. If it is removed it cannot be replaced and its birdlife will not be able to live elsewhere. ▼

Program: CROWKEY

This program uses the key in the flowchart to identify the members of the crow family. The program should be used with the CAPS LOCK on.

Type the program in and debug it so that it runs properly. Save the program on cassette.

```
 10 MODE1
 20 VDU23;8202;0;0;0;
 30 PROCVARS
 40 VDU19,2,4,0,0,0
 50 COLOUR3:COLOUR130:CLS
 60 PRINT TAB(2,2)"**** Key : Cro
w (Corvid) family ****"
 70 VDU28,4,28,35,5
 80 N=1:COLOUR131:CLS:COLOUR129
 90 PRINT TAB(1,20)" Press Y for
Yes or N for No. "
100 COLOUR131
110 REPEAT
120   PROCQ
130   UNTIL L<1
140 COLOUR1
150 PRINT TAB(2,10);:IF L=0 THEN
PRINT" This bird is a "A$(N) ELSE
PRINT"    Not a member of the crow
family found wild in Britain."
160 COLOUR3:COLOUR128
170 PRINT TAB(1,20)"       Another
 go (Y/N) ?         "
180 A$=GET$:IF A$="" THEN 180
190 IF A$="Y" THEN 80
200 IF A$="N" THEN MODE7:STOP ELS
E 180


210 DEFPROCVARS
220 DIMA$(21)
230 A$(1)="09Is the bird all (or
mainly) black ?02"
240 A$(2)="03Is it grey and black
 ?04"
250 A$(3)="hooded crow."
260 A$(4)="05Is it white and blac
k ?06"
270 A$(5)="magpie."
280 A$(6)="07Is it partly pink wi
th blue wing patches and white rump
 ?08"
```

```
290 A$(7)="jay."
300 A$(8)="-1"
310 A$(9)="15Has it a black bill
?10"
320 A$(10)="11Does it have a silv
er-white bill ?12"
330 A$(11)="rook."
340 A$(12)="13Does it have a red
bill ?14"
350 A$(13)="chough."
360 A$(14)="-1"
370 A$(15)="21Does it have a grey
nape and pale eyes ?16"
380 A$(16)="17Is it large with a
heavy bill and wedge-shaped tail?18
"
390 A$(17)="raven."
400 A$(18)="19Has it a rounded ta
il ?20"
410 A$(19)="carrion crow."
420 A$(20)="-1"
430 A$(21)="jackdaw."
440 ENDPROC


450 DEFPROCQ
460 COLOUR0
470 X$=MID$(A$(N),3,LENA$(N)-4)
480 PRINT TAB(2,10);
490 IF LENX$<28 THEN 550
500 W=30
510 REPEAT
520   W=W-1
530   UNTIL MID$(X$,W,1)=" "
540 X$=LEFT$(X$,W)+STRING$(32-W,"
")+MID$(X$,W+1)
550 PRINTX$
560 A$=GET$:IF A$="" THEN 560
570 IF A$<>"Y" AND A$<>"N" THEN 5
60
580 PRINT TAB(4,10)STRING$(LENX$,
" ")
590 IF A$="Y" THEN N=VAL(LEFT$(A$
(N),2))
600 IF A$="N" THEN N=VAL(RIGHT$(A
$(N),2))
610 L=VAL(LEFT$(A$(N),2))
620 ENDPROC
```

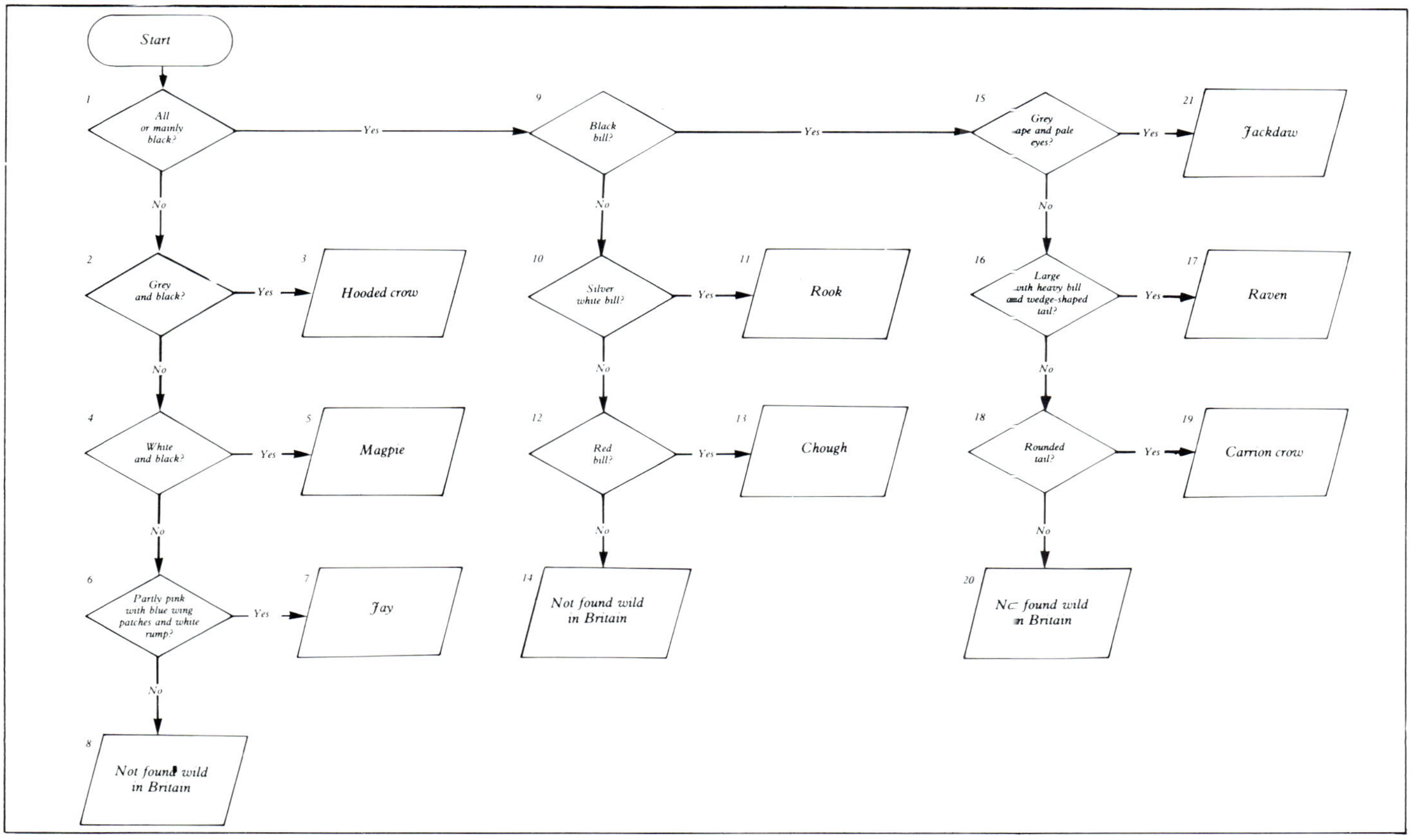

Flowchart

Start

1. All or mainly black? — Yes → 9. Black bill? — Yes → 15. Grey nape and pale eyes? — Yes → 21. Jackdaw

1. No ↓
2. Grey and black? — Yes → 3. Hooded crow
2. No ↓
4. White and black? — Yes → 5. Magpie
4. No ↓
6. Partly pink with blue wing patches and white rump? — Yes → 7. Jay
6. No ↓
8. Not found wild in Britain

9. No ↓
10. Silver white bill? — Yes → 11. Rook
10. No ↓
12. Red bill? — Yes → 13. Chough
12. No ↓
14. Not found wild in Britain

15. No ↓
16. Large with heavy bill and wedge-shaped tail? — Yes → 17. Raven
16. No ↓
18. Rounded tail? — Yes → 19. Carrion crow
18. No ↓
20. Not found wild in Britain

About this program

1. This program is an example of a key. It uses questions requiring a yes or no answer, and it is based on the flowchart. The diamond-shaped boxes are for questions; the parallelogram-shaped boxes are for information. The box numbers are used when the flowchart is converted into a program. The computer refers to each box by its number.

2. In MODE 1 there are four colours available: black, 0; red, 1; yellow, 2; and white, 3. Line 40 changes yellow (2) to blue (2). Line 50 sets the foreground colour to white (3) and the background colour to blue (2). The background colour number is 128 plus the colour number. In this case 128+2=130. CLS will now make the whole screen blue. Line 70 creates a text window. Its size and position are defined by the four numbers following VDU 28. Everything is now printed within the area of the text window. Try this short program. It illustrates a different text window.

```
10  MODE1
20  VDU28,10,22,29,11
30  REPEAT
40    PRINT"text window"
50  UNTIL FALSE
```

3. Lines 210–440 give a procedure to fill the array A$ with the words in the boxes of the flowchart. It is given the name DEFPROCVARS.

The information about each box is entered as a line of program. An example is given below:

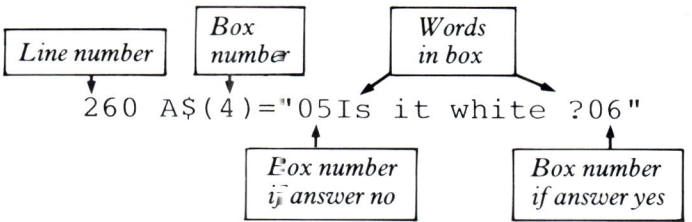

```
260 A$(4)="05Is it white ?06"
```

Inside the inverted commas it is necessary to write box numbers with one digit with a zero in front. When the computer reads a −1 for the next box number, then "Not found living wild in Britain" is printed.

Changes you can make

1. Try using the program for a different family of birds, such as the thrush or tit family. First make a flowchart similar to the one shown, you will need to choose suitable questions to describe the family. Number each of the boxes. Now alter the program as follows:
Line 60: change the title.
Line 220: change DIMA$(21) so that the number in brackets equals the number of boxes in your flowchart. Fill the array A$(1), A$(2) . . . with your data.

2. Try using this program for a different subject such as trees, cars or sports.

Bird words

Adaptation Changing to fit the *environment*. Part of *evolution*.

Barb A branch off the main shaft of a feather which carries hooked barbules that link adjacent barbs together.

Barbule See *barb*.

Behaviour An activity linked to a special purpose, e.g. breeding behaviour or feeding behaviour.

Binoculars An optical device enabling you to use both eyes to view a bird at a distance.

Bird of prey A bird which feeds on animals. Usually refers to eagles, hawks and falcons, also owls.

Bird recorder A person who keeps records of birds seen in an area. See under Bird books.

Breeding season The period during which birds reproduce, usually during the spring and summer.

Brood The young birds hatched from a *clutch* of eggs.

Clutch A set of eggs laid by a female bird. Some birds lay more than one clutch in a *breeding season*.

Colony A group of birds breeding together.

Coniferous Describes a tree which bears cones, e.g. a pine.

Conservation Preserving the natural *environment* by limiting the effects of people's use of it.

Courtship The establishment of a bond between a male and a female bird, often using display, resulting in eventual nesting.

Coverts Small feathers which cover the base of larger ones, e.g. *wing coverts* or *tail coverts*. *Ear coverts* cover the ear openings.

Deciduous Describes a tree which loses its leaves in winter.

Display Special *behaviour* often using bright *plumage*. Used during *courtship* and to defend *territory*.

Drumming The bill-tapping of a woodpecker on a dead branch, part of its *display*.

Ear coverts See *coverts*.

Environment All of the external influences on a living thing, e.g. weather, temperature, *habitat*.

Estuary The lower end of a river, where it meets the sea. At low tide mud and sand provide feeding areas for *wading birds*.

Evolution The gradual changing of an organism over a long period of time.

Eye ring A coloured ring around the eye.

Field guide A pocket-sized book that can easily be carried outside to help in the identification of birds.

Flight line A line followed by birds flying between feeding areas and a *roost*.

Food chain A link between plants and animals using feeding. If a caterpillar eats a plant, and is itself eaten by a blue tit which is then killed by a sparrowhawk, the chain would be plant-caterpillar-tit-hawk.

Generic name Part of the *scientific name* given to a *species* which indicates the *genus* to which the species belongs. Blue tits belong to the *genus Parus*, blackbirds to the *genus Turdus*.

Genus See *generic name*.

Habitat The place where a living thing lives. Examples are *woodland*, *heaths*, *moors* and *wetlands*.

Heath A *habitat* type with heather, gorse and scattered trees and bushes.

Incubation The warming of an egg by the parent bird, essential to the development of the chick.

Migration The movement of a *population* of birds between breeding grounds and wintering grounds.

Moorland A *habitat* type without trees, usually with heather and boggy areas.

Moult The replacement of old feathers by new ones, usually at the end of the *breeding season*. Some feathers may also be moulted before breeding.

Nature reserve An area of land set aside for *conservation* usually owned or managed by a conservation body.

Nest box An artificial nest site, often made of wood, frequently for hole-nesting birds.

Nestling A young bird still in the nest.

Organochlorides Chemicals often used in pesticides. Many are particularly poisonous to wildlife.

Ornithologist A person who studies birds and their *behaviour*.

Plumage The feathers covering a bird's body.

Pollution The introduction into the *environment* of unnatural and harmful substances, e.g. oil.

Population A group of birds which live in a particular area or *habitat*.

Predator An animal which feeds on other animals.

Primary One of the outer feathers of the wing, used for flying.

Resident A bird which remains within an area throughout the year.

Roost The place where birds sleep. Some birds, like starlings, have roosts where thousands of birds sleep together.

Rump A bird's upper parts just above the tail.

Scientific name An internationally recognized name consisting of a *generic name* followed by a *specific name*.

Seabird A bird which spends most of its life at sea.

Secondary One of the inner wing feathers, used for flying.

Site of Special Scientific Interest An important natural area which is not a *nature reserve*, but is officially recognized.

Song Sounds produced by a bird to attract a mate or announce a *territory*.

Song post A prominent place from which a bird sings, often to denote its *territory*.

Species A population which is sufficiently different from other populations that they do not breed together. Each species has an individual *scientific name*.

Specific name Part of the *scientific name* given to a *species*, which identifies it from other *species* in the same *genus*. Blue tits are called *Parus caeruleus*, great tits are *Parus major*. The *specific name* always comes after the *generic name*.

Summer visitor A bird which comes to an area to breed and migrates away for the winter.

Tail coverts See *coverts*.

Territory An area defended by a bird in which it will breed or feed.

Wading bird A type of bird usually found in *wetland* areas and *estuaries*, often with long legs.

Wetland An area of freshwater which includes rivers, lakes, canals and marshes.

Wing bar A coloured line across the wing seen in flight or at rest.

Wing coverts Small feathers which cover the base of the *primary* and *secondary* feathers.

Wing span The distance between wing tips with the wings spread out.

Winter visitor A bird which comes to an area for the winter and migrates away to breed.

Woodland A *habitat* type made up of trees which could be *deciduous* or *coniferous*.

Bird books

Bird Count, H. M. Dobinson, Penguin, 1976. (Bird projects)
Watching Birds, I. Wallace, Usborne, 1982. (For beginners)
Discover Birds, I. Wallace, Whizzard/Andre Deutsch, 1979. (For beginners)
Birdwatchers' Yearbook 1984, J. Pemberton, Buckingham Press, 1983. (Details of bird reserves, bird recorders, bird clubs, and conservation bodies)
Birdwatching, G. Thomas, Piccolo, 1983. (For beginners with projects)
The RSPB Book of British Birds, P. Holden, J. T. R. Sharrock, H. Burn, Macmillan, 1982. (Field guide)
A Field Guide to the Birds of Britain and Europe, R T. Peterson, G. Mountfort, P. A. D. Hollom, Collins, 1983. (Field guide)
The Shell Guide to the Birds of Britain and Ireland, J. Ferguson-Lees, I. Willis, J. T. R. Sharrock, Michael Joseph, 1983. (Field guide)
The Birds of Britain and Europe, H. Heinzel, R. S. R. Fitter, J. Parslow, Collins, 1972. (Field guide)
Nestboxes, J. Flegg, D. Glue, British Trust for Ornithology, 1971. (How to make nest boxes)

Bird addresses

Royal Society for the Protection of Birds, The Lodge, Sandy, Bedfordshire SG19 2DL
Young Ornithologists' Club, The Lodge, Sandy, Bedfordshire SG19 2DL
British Trust for Ornithology, Beech Grove, Tring, Hertfordshire HP23 5NR

Computer words

Keywords in this list are defined for the BBC microcomputer. Other machines use similar, but not necessarily identical keywords.

BASIC The language most commonly used by microcomputers. The word comes from the first letters of the phrase, Beginners All-purpose Symbolic Instruction Code. BASIC is a high level language because it uses words similar to human language. Different makes of microcomputer operate different dialects of BASIC. This means that programs written for one make of machine will not run on another make.

CHAIN A *command* which enables a program to LOAD and RUN automatically. Programs are selected by a *file name*. The name must be put in inverted commas. For example, CHAIN "ANAGRAMS".

CHAIN"" A *command* which will LOAD and RUN the next program from tape regardless of the *file name*.

COLOUR A statement which selects the colour for both text and its background as displayed on the screen.

Command A word which the computer acts on immediately it is typed in at the keyboard.

CLG A statement which clears the graphics window.

CLS A statement which clears the text window. The text window may not be the same as the graphics window.

Data Information that must be available in a program for the program to do its job. For example, in a bird quiz the questions and their answers could be stored as DATA statements.

Database A program rather like a card index file that allows you to store facts about a subject. The facts can be sorted and analysed by asking questions of the program that uses the database.

DEFPROC This word is used in a program to tell the computer that a procedure will now be defined. The procedure is given a name which describes its contents. For example, DEFPROCBIRD might be a procedure for a bird symbol. At the end of the procedure ENDPROC is used to let the computer know it has reached the end.

DELETE A *command* which erases a line, or group of lines, from a program. For example, DELETE 60,90 would remove all lines from 60 to 90 inclusive.

DIM A statement which tells the computer to set up an array. An array is like a street of numbered houses. Letters can be posted through each door. Arrays are given names which describe the contents. For example, DIM size (21) could be an array containing the sizes of 21 different birds.

DRAW A statement which allows lines to be drawn on the screen.

END This tells the computer that it has reached the end of the program.

GCOL A statement which sets the colour of the graphics in a program.

File name The name given to a program when it is stored on tape or disc.

INPUT A means of entering information into the computer whilst a program is running. For example,
340 PRINT "How old are you";
350 INPUT age

Keyword A word that is part of the BASIC computer language.

LIST A *command* which makes the computer print out whatever program is in its memory. A long list runs off the top of the screen too quickly for reading. By pressing CTRL and then pressing N whilst still holding down CTRL, the list will appear a screenful at a time. This is called paging. The next page is printed by pressing SHIFT.

LOAD This is a *command* which will load a program into memory from tape or disc. Programs are selected by a *file name*. This name must be enclosed in inverted commas. For example, LOAD "ANAGRAMS".

LOAD"" This is a *command* that will load the next program on a tape regardless of the *file name*.

MODE A statement which selects the amount of graphics and text allowed on the screen.

MOVE A statement which moves the graphics cursor without drawing a line.

PRINT A statement telling the computer to print words on the screen. The words are enclosed in inverted commas and follow the PRINT statement.
For example,
PRINT "How old are you?"
PRINT by itself will leave a blank line.

REM A marker which can be put into a program. It does not affect the way the program runs, but it allows reference information to be put into the listing.
For example,
10 REM Pinewood Programming 1984

RENUMBER A *command* which will renumber your program giving the first line 10, the second line 20, and so on. RENUMBER 900 will renumber your program starting at line 900.

RUN A statement which tells the computer to follow the program instructions in numerical order.

SAVE A *command* which tells the computer to save a program on tape or disc. The program must be given a *file name* of up to 10 characters for tape. It must start with a letter and must not contain spaces or punctuation marks, but must be enclosed in inverted commas. For example, SAVE "HABITAT"

Simulation A program which attempts to describe a changing situation. For example, a program of a space flight.

Computer books

Write your own Adventure Programs for your Computer, Jenny Tyler, Les Howarth, Usborne, 1983.
Understanding the Micro, Judy Tatchell, Bill Bennett, Usborne, 1982.
Micro Knowledge, John Smith, Ladybird, 1984.
Projects for Programs, Derek Blease, Ladybird, 1984.
Micros are Fun, Tony Gray, Carl Bilson, Ladybird, 1984.
Ideas for Micro Users, Tony Gray, Carl Bilson, Ladybird, 1984.
Whizz Kids Computers. Derrick Daines, Macdonald, 1983.

Computer addresses

Both of these organisations are voluntary. Please include a stamped and addressed envelope when sending for information.

Association of Computer Clubs, c/o Rupert Steele, 17 Lawrie Park Crescent, London SE26 6HH
Computer Town UK, c/o Margaret Spooner, Personal Computer World, 62 Oxford Street, London W1A 2HG

Software

These programs are databases developed for children to use. The first two use a card index approach and can be used for projects suggested on page 17 and page 34. The other program has a tree structure and could be used for more work on identification, see page 42.

Factfile, Cambridge Micro Software, 1982. (Available for BBC, Spectrum, RML 480Z)
Quest, AUCBE, 1983. (Available for BBC, RML 480Z)

Tree of Knowledge, Acornsoft, 1982. (Available for BBC, Electron)

Use the space below to make notes about software you find useful for bird projects.

Index